"A BOOK THAT EARNS THE PRAISE, I COULDN'T PUT IT DOWN...

"Against the advice of military authorities, Johnson insisted on flying with a B-26 of the 22nd Bomber Group on a mission over New Guinea, one of the most dangerous targets in the South Pacific at that time.

"Shortly before reaching the target, the plane lost a generator and had to drop out of formation. Two of the craft's guns would not function properly.

"The lone plane was pounced upon by eight Japanese Zeros and riddled with machine-gun fire. The attackers included Saburo Saki, one of the greatest fighter pilots in history . . ."

—LOUISVILLE TIMES

MARTIN CAIDIN is one of the outstanding aviation and astronautics authorities in the world. He has twice, in 1958 and 1961, won the Aviation/Space Writers Association award as the outstanding author in the field of aviation. Mr. Caidin also wrote EVERYTHING BUT THE FLAK, published in paperback by Popular Library.

EDWARD HYMOFF, a prolific writer on military and aerospace subjects, has wide experience in both his specialties. He has flown missions with SAC bombers, has covered all the manned space flights at Cape Kennedy, and has lectured widely on military and space events. Mr. Hymoff is a former news editor for NBC.

THE MISSION

Martin Caidin and Edward Hymoff

POPULAR LIBRARY—NEW YORK

ACKNOWLEDGMENTS

Without the unstinting help of . . .

General Samuel E. Anderson, USAF (Ret.); Harry G. Baren; Master Sergeant Howard W. Clark, USAF; Gerald J. Crosson; Tom Cunningham; Dwight Divine II; Brigadier General John N. Ewbank, Jr., USAF; James V. Fahy; Raymond J. Flanagan; Colonel Louis W. Ford, USAF; Pat Frank; Walter Gaylor; James M. Hafey; Woodrow W. Harrison; William B. Harwood; Hoffman Laboratories, Inc.; Seiji Ishikawa; Robert Ivy; Lieutenant Colonel Paul Kelly, U. S. Army; Michael Kobylarz; Walter A. Krell; Colonel Leon G. Lewis, USAF; A. B. Livingston; Colonel Hugh B. Manson, USAF; Calvin M. Markham; Robert Marshall; Claude A. McCredie; Senior Master Sergeant George E. McGowan, USAF; James Merritt; William K. Miller; Foster Mitchell; Booth Mooney; Tadashi Nakajima; Frederick C. Nichols; Philip North; Robertson M. Pearson; Charles L. Pierce; Group Captain H. R. Rayner, R.A.A.F.; John L. Richardson; Dominic Rio; Pat Robinson; Major General Ralph Royce, USAF (Ret.); Saburo Sakai; Fred Saito; Masahisa Saito; Brigadier General Martin F. Scanlon, USAF (Ret.); Walter H. Schoeneck; Frederick Schroeder; George Shaw; John F. Shepherd; Arthur L. Smith; Allan Staley; Albert Stanwood; Captain Francis R. Stevens, Jr., U. S. Army; Mrs. Francis Robert Stevens; Lyle E. Thompson; Wilson B. Waddy; Lillis M. Walker; Milton Weiner; William Westland; Bennie O. Westmoreland; Hajima Yoshida, and Lieutenant Samuel Young, U. S. Army.

. . . this book would not have been possible.

CONTENTS

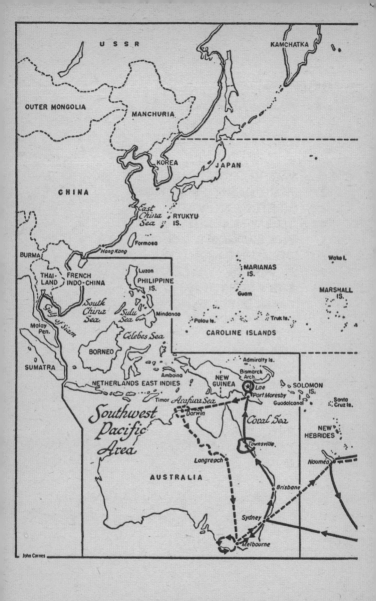

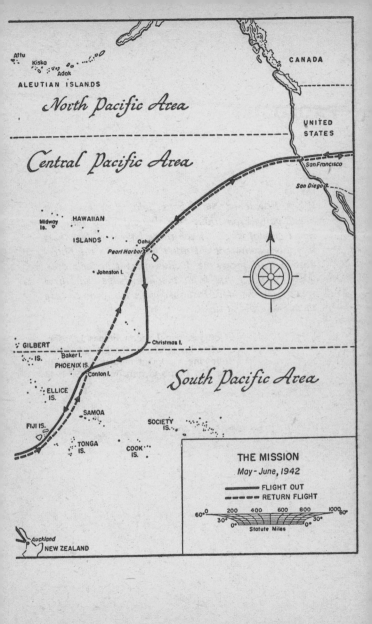

PROLOGUE

When I watched those boys fighting to keep that plane going, something was burned deep into me that I cannot forget. When those boys and the others like them come back, I don't want to see the bitterness in their faces, the disillusionment in their eyes, which would come from the knowledge that there was something more I might have tried to do to help them—and didn't do it.

Congressman Lyndon Baines Johnson,
after his return to the United States,
following a combat mission flown with
the 22d Bomb Group on June 9, 1942

CHAPTER ONE

WASHINGTON, 1941

At eleven o'clock on the morning of December 8, 1941, helmeted marines in greatcoats moved swiftly to assigned positions on and about Capitol Hill. They moved briskly in double time, heels thudding against the cold pavement, bayonets gleaming brightly at the end of rifles held at the ready.

Other men also took up positions of guard. Some were Army troops who dropped from the backs of trucks at street corners. Others wore civilian clothes: Secret Service men with riot guns poised. And there were grim-faced District police.

The United States prepared to go to war. Several thousand miles to the west, Pearl Harbor lay in shambles. On the morning of December 7, 1941, some crude leaflets had fluttered down on the flaming island of Oahu. They read: GODDAMN AMERICANS ALL GO TO HELL. These ludicrous papers that fell to the ground at Pearl Harbor came to rest in the midst of shocking reality. More than four thousand Americans were dead or wounded by Japanese bombs and by explosions aboard stricken ships and planes and at shore installations. The United States Navy alone lost more men within two hours than it had yielded to its enemies in two previous wars. Before the first day of the war ended, the United States had lost two-thirds of all its aircraft in the Pacific, and had lost superiority in the air to the Japanese.

On the morning of December 8, 1941, the nation's capital set itself the urgent task of binding together the fibers of national strength. Congressmen, faces mirroring their emotions, moved quickly to their offices on this first Monday of war.

Telegrams from the families and relatives of servicemen who were stationed at Pearl Harbor were already arriving in large numbers. Each message was different and yet each was the same. Each begged to know whether someone was alive, or dead, or wounded.

Like many other legislators, Congressman Lyndon Baines Johnson of Austin, Texas, faced the task of noting these telegrams filled with unspoken anguish and of being unable to offer assurances of the safety of relatives in the area of attack. The release of initial casualty lists increased the pressure upon Congressmen. Johnson's staff directed specific inquiries to the War Department.

Grim headlines were the order of the day in the newspapers that were placed on Lyndon Johnson's desk. Able to read swiftly and accurately, the tall Texan digested the details of the historic events engulfing him and those about him. Pushing the papers aside, he hurried his work to prepare for the joint session of the Congress, scheduled for 12:30 P.M.

Through the window of Congressman Johnson's office could be seen workmen pounding stakes into the ground and stringing wire cables around the House wing of the Capitol. At the same time, other men were raising barricades before the main entrances, and attendants were placing at all entranceways freshly painted signs that proclaimed: SHOW YOUR PASSES.

Approximately at noon Johnson left the House Office Building for the Capitol. A new world faced him: armed guards blocked his entrance, and marines and soldiers stood with fixed bayonets in front of every doorway and at the ground-floor windows. Before him a guard snapped to port arms. Cold eyes examined Johnson's credentials; he was then politely ushered past the first barrier. But he had to pass two more guards before he could reach the House chamber.

Within the chamber itself the undercurrent of conversation was uncommonly subdued. Men gathered briefly in groups, their heads bent together; others, many more than was usual, sat somberly in their chairs, reflecting on the disintegration of the old world and the great, unknown dangers of the new. Then the Senators were all present and in their seats. Presently, in solemn movement, the members of the Supreme Court, garbed in flowing black robes, took their seats along the edge of the well of the House, to the left of the rostrum.

At 12:23 P.M. the members of the President's Cabinet arrived. Precisely at that moment a gavel rapped sharply. House Speaker Sam Rayburn with this move commanded silence.

His deep voice boomed out: "The President of the United States!"

Immediately the assembled throng rose to its feet, members of both Houses, guests in the rear of the chamber, diplomats in the gallery, officials of the government, soldiers, and the few privileged visitors in the galleries all rising like a breaking wave to stand before the arriving President.

For a moment there hung a thick and heavy silence; abruptly it vanished in a roar of spontaneous applause. Not even Sam Rayburn and his gavel could stem the ovation that burst forth to shake the great room. Franklin Delano Roosevelt for more than a minute waited before the cheering and shouting and the booming applause; nothing in his eight years as Chief Executive rivaled the spirited, tumultuous outcry.

As the outpouring of confidence in the Chief died down, the Chaplain spoke, not quickly, perhaps, but because of the press of the moment, briefly. President Roosevelt spoke for six and one-half minutes. His sentences, ringing and clearly enunciated, were punctured repeatedly by outbreaks of wild applause. His voice lashed out. It drilled into the hearing of all present the names of lands already suffering the blows of Japanese steel. One by one, in staccato fashion, they came: the Philippines, Midway, Wake, Guam, Pearl Harbor, Hong Kong, Malaya, and, still others.

The phrase that all Americans and much of the world would come to know so well rang out in clarion tones: "We will gain the inevitable triumph, so help us God."

And then there was the culmination of the brief, emotional address, the request of the President to the Congress:

"I ask that the Congress declare that since the unprovoked and dastardly attack by Japan on Sunday, December 7, a state of war has existed between the United States and the Japanese Empire."

The movie lights blazed down from the galleries as a massed roar inundated the room. Among those who added to the applause was Congressman Lyndon Johnson, "protégé" of this same President. He thought ahead to his plans for the future, for he was about to leave this chamber, his offices, and the capital itself. During the ensuing days, Congressman Johnson was to make clear his decision to his fellow representatives.

The members of the House of Representatives on December 11, 1941, assembled in their chamber. There was an air of grim attention. Speaker Rayburn stood before them to read the Presidential request that the Congress "recognize a state of war between the United States and Germany, and between the United States and Italy." [1] Like the muffled beat of a drum came the slow and methodical roll call for the declaration of war against Germany.

One hour later, Lyndon Johnson rose to his feet. He requested that the Chair recognize him: "Mr. Speaker!"

His voice commanded attention. "I ask unanimous consent for an indefinite leave of absence."

Speaker Sam Rayburn nodded to his fellow Texan. He then raised his eyes and his gaze swept the chamber.

"Is there objection to the request of the gentleman from Texas?" The members of the Congress remained silent; it was unanimous acceptance of the request. [2]

Speaker Rayburn's gavel rapped smartly in the sign of permission granted to the request. "So be it."

NOTE: Superior figures refer to Notes and Sources at end of text.

Congressman Johnson gathered together the papers on his desk. He rose again to his feet and clasped the hands offered by the representatives closest to him. Then, quickly, he strode from the chamber and returned to his office to attend to final details at his desk.

Within the hour Congressman Johnson, for several years a lieutenant commander in the United States Naval Reserve, requested that he be called by the Navy to active duty.

Three days later, he was officially in uniform, the first member of the House of Representatives to assume an active military role.

CHAPTER TWO

ASSIGNMENT FROM F.D.R.

Reporting for active duty only a few days after Pearl Harbor, Lieutenant Commander L. B. Johnson "was ordered to the Office of the Chief of Naval Operations, Navy Department, Washington, D.C., for instruction . . ." [3] The Navy planned to use Johnson's unique talents as a legislator to assist in the critical task of building up the organizational structure through which would flow men and matériel from the United States into the Pacific. It was a task that demanded not only administrative and organizational detail but also—and equally as important—the ability to deal with diplomatic problems that could easily snag military moves, which demanded speed and freedom of execution. In the Pacific and Asian areas especially, the rapid conquests of Japan had thrown government after government into the unhappy position of being in exile in friendly and still free countries. These nations represented, often, sovereign states with their own ideas; having been embroiled in fighting through their status as possessions or commonwealth members of European powers, they had drawn firm conclusions as to the manner in which the fight against the Japanese should be prosecuted. This posed a dilemma for the United States, which realized clearly that it would and must bear the major part of the task of stopping the Japanese and ultimately hurling them back from their newly won positions.

But it was not possible simply to step into the breach and with a flourish of military strength assume both leadership and command (the two are quite distinct). Diplomatic relations still had to move through their devious channels, a task complicated by the raw wounds and seared pride of the defeated. At the same time the United States was hardly in the position to proclaim its superiority in knowledge and leadership, having suffered a series of devastating blows at the hands of the Japanese.

Immediately upon completion of his training in Washington, Lieutenant Commander Johnson received his orders to report at once to Headquarters, Twelfth Naval District, in San Francisco, California. His assignment was directly to the Office of the Chief, United States–New Zealand Navy Command.

Among the facts of life concerning the "command" relationship between the United States and New Zealand was the unhappy realization that the government of New Zealand had much less faith in the United States Navy than we were expressing in our press dispatches at the time. There had already been a series of command structures in the Pacific, and the one that promised the greatest hope, ABDA (American-British-Dutch-Australian), toppled helplessly when the Japanese swarmed into Singapore in February and then fired an invasion force into Java. The Dutch commander-in-chief in the Netherlands East Indies picked up the broken pieces of command, but these fell apart when the Dutch and American defenses in Java collapsed and the survivors fled for their lives.

On March 9, 1942, President Roosevelt cabled to Winston Churchill that "The Pacific situation is now very grave" [4]—as indeed it was. A reappraisal of the defense of New Zealand by that government noted that the United States Navy was "responsible for the protection of New Zealand. This would have made the New Zealand Government much less apprehensive about the security of New Zealand had that navy not been so severely crippled at Pearl Harbour." [5]

The need for diplomatic finesse in the negotiations between the United States government, through its naval command, and the government of New Zealand was especially emphasized by New Zealand's concern over command structure as well as by its fears concerning the weakness of the American naval forces in the Pacific.

In mid-March, 1942, a new command structure was again established. The British were handed the Indian Ocean and the Middle East for which to fight, and the United States shouldered the responsibility for the entire Pacific—including Australia and New Guinea. However, a further breakdown of the structure only added to the cumulative unhappiness of the New Zealanders, who noted that they had been "placed in a different command from Australia. The New Zealand Government did not fully approve of the separation as it had always considered that Australia and New Zealand should be regarded as a strategic whole, but in view of the urgent necessity for finalising some arrangement it acquiesced." [6]

Commander Johnson found the assignment to the United States–New Zealand Navy Command not at all to his liking. He had not left the chambers of the Congress simply to shift from his desk in Washington, D.C., across the country to another desk in San Francisco. He had asked for active duty —he made this very clear to his superiors—in order to be assigned to a combat theater, not the waters of San Francisco Bay. His repeated requests for overseas assignment, however, produced no results.

Who wanted to be responsible for sending a Congressman off to be killed, especially when the analytical mind of that Congressman, skilled in the ways of politics and high-level relationships, was of great value to the United States in its dealings with other countries?

Johnson fretted about the obstacles in his path and finally decided to take matters into his own hands. "Between trains" en route to Washington, he visited for several hours with his brother, Sam Houston Johnson, who was then working in Denver. Johnson was eloquent in voicing his unhappiness over the situation: he had had enough of Stateside duty.

"I'm not finding out anything about the war," he complained. "I'm not doing anything. I would be worth more to the country in Congress than I am in this assignment. I'm going to Washington and talk to the Boss. He's got to get something done about me." [7]

In Washington soon afterward, Johnson lost no time securing an appointment with the President at the White House. There he explained his reasons for wanting to obtain an overseas assignment, to get out in the field where he would be able to find out what the war was really like, and, above all, to be able to serve in a manner he considered truly useful.

That meeting was to have far-reaching effects that neither President Roosevelt nor Congressman-Commander Johnson could possibly foresee. It would result in a trip equivalent to circling the earth around the equator and would subject the Congressman to combat hazards so severe that a general officer of the United States Army would be directed to keep that same young Congressman out of a bomber in which he was determined to fly over Japanese-held territory.

Commander Johnson could not have approached "the Boss" at a time better guaranteed to obtain what he wanted, and more. For not only was the President involved in a bitter controversy between nations but he also was being forced to settle differences between his own top military commanders in the Pacific whose personal antagonisms were so severe that they were compromising the unity of the forces arrayed against the Japanese.

It had become more and more difficult for the nation's Commander-in-Chief to determine what was really happening in the remote Southwest Pacific. Personal animosities that riddled the command structure were making it virtually impossible to distinguish between "hard" fact and "emphasized" fact. Reports reaching the Presidential desk often were greatly condensed in such a way as to disguise actual conditions, and omissions of "minor factors" often served to becloud the overall picture.

The strong national pride of our Pacific allies made it difficult for us to gauge their ability to defend themselves against the Japanese, while controversy between honest and well-meaning, but diametrically opposed, leaders of different nations made it equally difficult to arrive at decisions for action in the Southwest Pacific Area (SWPA). The fact that General Douglas MacArthur was arriving in Australia with only defeat to show for all his efforts to defend the Philippines added nothing to our own prestige among our allies.

What was needed was an objective viewpoint—one that would be scrupulously honest and wholly impartial and represent the need of the President to learn the truth about events taking place on the other side of the world. With his well-established powers of observation, his brilliantly analytical mind, his talents at discovering the true nature of complex situations—all sharpened on the whetstone of harsh political experience—Lyndon B. Johnson fitted the needs of President Roosevelt perfectly. His own close friendship with and loyalty to the President, the fact that he was already a commissioned naval officer on active duty, his chafing to get away from his desk and to the combat theater—all these factors dropped neatly into place and permitted President Roosevelt to appoint Commander Johnson as his personal representative on a long survey mission of the South and Southwest areas of the Pacific theater of combat.

Delighted with his assignment, Johnson remained in Washington only long enough to take care of some last-minute details. He spent some time in his own office in the old House Office Building. His wife, Lady Bird, was in charge there, for she had assumed the role of unsalaried stand-in in order to keep the work of the office moving as much as was possible. Johnson himself—immediately on reaching active-duty status —had notified the House Sergeant-at-Arms that while he was serving actively in the Navy he would not accept the customary congressional salary of ten thousand dollars a year. Instead, he would receive only the three thousand dollars annually paid to an officer of his rank.[8]

He returned to San Francisco to begin preparations for his long journey across the Pacific. He also began to examine more deeply, and with a specific purpose in mind, the intricacies of command and the conflicts that were undermining the strength of our limited combat forces in the Pacific, paying special attention to the SWPA. Australia was the haven of the vanquished—Americans and many of other nationalities—and it was there that the seeds of difficulty were sprouting.

". . . the key importance of Australia to plans for containing the Japanese had been recognized, and its loss, or even the loss of any considerable part of it, obviously might call into question the whole of the defensive strategy agreed upon for the Pacific. Australia herself was unequal to the task of providing her own defense." [9]

Official histories are universally consistent in making special note that "In the air especially, the burden of defending Australia would have to fall upon the Americans. . . . Upon the Americans, too, would fall the main responsibility for defense of the island chain running back from Australia to provide and shield a line of communication with the United States." [10]

All this—as Lyndon Johnson prepared for his special mission—was a problem existing under conditions that have been described as identical to the disadvantages that had beset the efforts of the Americans and their allies first in the Philippines and then in the Netherlands East Indies, where—it was remembered with acute discomfort—we had collectively been whipped by the Japanese invader. In Australia it seemed to be, once again, a matter of men who "worked against time, enjoyed few of the benefits of previous preparation, and improvised as they went, in a backbreaking attempt to meet the changing requirements of a highly fluid tactical situation." [11]

Above all, there were the basic organizational problems. These alone were proving a crippling factor to our combat operations against the Japanese. Official histories note that "the Americans were dependent upon the Australians for communications and were forced to rely heavily upon them in all matters of administration; and once more good will on both sides was in itself insufficient to overcome all the difficulties." [12]

It was noted, but the knowledge was carefully guarded, especially at that time, that "the Americans and Australians had their backs to the wall and were faced with the threat of increasing enemy pressure, not only from the northwest but also from the northeast." [13]

There was also a particularly ominous appraisal of the situation in the SWPA—one that affected directly the decision to send Lyndon Johnson to that area—which noted that "for the moment the Air Corps units in Australia were not at all certain of their future. In this period of uncertainty the Secretary of War could well state that 'circumstances will determine the extent and nature of future United States air operations in the Southwest Pacific Area,' but the American airmen and their commanding officers in Australia wondered just what those circumstances would be." [14]

Wonder about the same problems and the "uncertainty of circumstances," it has been shown, existed also in the White House—and specifically paved the way for the mission that Johnson was to make.

An exhaustive survey of official documents, several of which have not yet seen public light, reveals that well into the spring of 1942 there still existed in both Washington and Australia serious conflict as to "urgent questions of command and organization" in fighting the Japanese. The term "conflict" is perhaps too mild, for the bitterness between American commanders that finally spilled into the open made it all too clear that personal invective was hindering drastically the effectiveness of our forces.

There was, first, the problem of *who* was to be placed in over-all command. The disruption of existing organizations "had left no provision for an overall command of Allied resistance to the southward thrust of the Japanese." [15]

While Washington officials read the secret and contradictory reports from the SWPA and went off on their own arguments, the Combined Chiefs of Staff were forced to push as rapidly as possible toward a workable solution that would define and assign true responsibility to the Air Force and the other services. Unfortunately, the Air Force units in Australia had come to grips with still another enemy they had badly underestimated. They "soon discovered that they had an enemy almost as formidable in the natural barriers to operations offered by the continent of Australia—the world's smallest continent and largest island. Those American airmen who, after surviving the Java campaign, tried to make their way from the west coast of Australia to Melbourne learned something of the difficulties of transportation—the inadequate railroads skirting the coast and the undeveloped roadways running through vast stretches of uninhabited land. The perplexing logistical problems occasioned by the geography, terrain, inadequate transportation and communications facilities, and certain governmental policies, however, did not lessen the necessity for defending Australia." [16]

Adding to this burden, serious disputes arose between the Americans, the Australians, and the Dutch as to who had the authority to control all the forces then in Australia and at the immediate outlying bases. For example, Lieutenant General George H. Brett was operating on the assumption that, because he was the top deputy for General MacArthur, all air forces operated under his direct control.

This proved to be more assumption than actuality. The Dutch, thrown off their home islands, disdained such an arrangement, and on April 11, 1942, the same day that Johnson left for Washington, D.C., General Van Oyen informed Brett in less than cordial terms that as far as he, Van Oyen, was concerned, the Dutch Admiral Helfrich, *not* Brett, would command the Dutch Air Forces in Australia. It was only one example of the broken authority that crippled our air effort at the time.

Once again the situation required the direct intervention of President Roosevelt. There exists no doubt that he appreciated what was happening, for in his meetings with Air Force leaders he showed irritation at their preoccupation with organizational rules and parliamentary procedures when they should have been concentrating all their energies against the Japanese. Finally, the President had no choice but to step in among the Combined Chiefs of Staff. He "offered a proposal" that there be a separate Southwest Pacific Area under the command of General Douglas MacArthur, who would establish *his* own staff arrangement.

By April 18, 1942, after major discussions with "all Allied Governments concerned," MacArthur assumed official supreme command of the SWPA.* At the same time, General Brett assumed the command of the Allied Air Forces. But if anyone in Washington felt that it was now time to sigh with relief—because there was a clear road at long last to an autonomous prosecution of the war—it would have been premature relief indeed. For there still loomed wide gaps between American and Australian commanders, and there existed, most unfortunately, a problem concerning General MacArthur and one of his own officers.

It was into this situation of divided authority, petty bickering, personal antagonism, and primitive operational conditions (to say nothing of a well-equipped, victorious, and aggressive enemy) that Commander Johnson was about to be thrust. And even as he completed final arrangements, the situation in the SWPA was going from bad to worse.

Part of the problem centered around MacArthur's dislike of General Brett. Despite his position as Commander of the Allied Air Forces, Brett often found himself hobbled by obstacles placed in his path by MacArthur's office.

In addition, "the Allied commander did not have complete control of the Royal Australian Air Force." Brett himself noted that all control of the R.A.A.F. was, in fact, taken from him, "due mainly to Australian political interference and sabotage." [17]

No one could question that, even under the best of circumstances, the task that General Brett faced would have been staggering. The nature of that task and the difficulties in im-

* But not without the great displeasure, as has been noted, of the government of New Zealand.

plementing Brett's responsibilities were to play a major role in the tour Lyndon Johnson was to make through this area. For in the SWPA it was the Air Force, more than any other fighting arm, that conducted combat operations against the Japanese. The Navy, busy with critical operations elsewhere, made only rare penetrations into the SWPA. The Army had been shattered by one defeat after another and could be built up again only in slow and back-breaking fashion. Moreover, why waste Army forces on any ambitious but likely-to-be-fatal, premature land offensive against the Japanese when they were needed desperately within Australia for the defense of that island continent? On this point, all parties agreed.

From his conversations with two close friends and with officers who were so tired and worn by defeat that bluntness in speech was their only method of talking, Lyndon Johnson was to learn of these circumstances. Of greater value, of course, would be his own observations of and participation in activities in Australia and in the combat zones.

He would, for example, see that Brett had his hands tied at almost every turn. Even the basic matter of supply was a nightmare. Distance, the lack of communications, and the widely varying procedures in carrying out everyday duties all combined to create a mass of problems. There was even the problem of "the absence of stock lists among combat units. Parts which were requisitioned by units in Port Moresby, for example, could not be readily sent from depots in Australia, since the requisitioning unit used the manufacturers' part numbers and the depots used only their own stock numbers. It was not unusual for a six-month period to pass before certain items were forwarded from depots. In view of such conditions, it is not surprising that almost complete dependence was placed on salvage for the supply of spare parts." † [18]

The foundation of any aerial offensive against the Japanese lay in the creation of suitable airdromes and landing fields in the SWPA. But the situation was critical. Streams of reports that went back to the States—and which in various condensed forms reached the desk of President Roosevelt—made it clear that the foundation contained more sand than cement. "The entire program of air base projects was delayed by the lack of proper tools and equipment, the scarcity of local labor, and the lack of sufficient aviation battalions." [19]

All this was to affect directly the itinerary and the mode of travel of Lyndon Johnson. Had not a word ever been said to

† Lyndon Johnson was to be presented with a bizarre demonstration of this when he personally witnessed a scene where a mob of crew chiefs descended *en masse* on a crippled bomber that crash-landed directly in front of Johnson: *before the dust settled, the men were stripping the plane of its parts.*

him by intelligence, staff, and other officers who briefed him, and even had he lacked the confidence of two close friends, his own keen powers of observation would have brought the matter to his attention.

Several men especially were to play an intimate role as Johnson conducted his tour for President Roosevelt (and few of them would know of his status at the time of their conversations with him). One of the most important of these men was, of course, General Brett himself. Then there was Major General Ralph Royce, a hard-hitting, blunt veteran of several decades of military flight, who only two days before he met Johnson was given command of the Northeast Sector of Australia (and who in turn sent Brigadier General Martin F. Scanlon directly to Port Moresby, New Guinea, to whip things into shape at our most advanced combat outpost, from which we raided the Japanese). These men and others were to either officially brief Lyndon Johnson or yield to him the hard, "behind-the-scenes" facts in confidential discussions.

Again and again, incidents took place that revealed the disharmony existing between MacArthur and Brett (and other general officers, but to a lesser degree). Australian observers —liaison officers in MacArthur's headquarters in Melbourne —who witnessed many encounters between these two men secretly kept "lively reports" of the scenes. Official documents of the R.A.A.F.[20] note that among the difficulties Brett faced "was the awkward relationship that had existed between himself and the Supreme Commander." It would be unreasonable not to expect Johnson to become quickly and deeply aware of the undercurrents that were such a disrupting influence in the SWPA command structure.

There was one incident in particular that determined the future of the MacArthur-Brett relationship; it took place as MacArthur arrived by train at Melbourne, where he was to make his headquarters. Until MacArthur's arrival in the city, Brett had been the senior commander of all the Southwest Pacific.

Performing as required by courtesy and protocol—to say nothing of their relationship—Brett inquired politely of MacArthur if he wished to be accompanied to his hotel. Officers present at the scene were shocked when MacArthur replied, "No," and drove off.

Still later, Generals Brett and Ralph Royce paid a formal call to the new commander. They were astonished when MacArthur refused to see them. Coldly, they left their cards.

"You'd think we were orderlies," Royce growled. "Or don't we belong to the right fraternity?"

Eight days passed before MacArthur finally received his ranking officer. Brett was stunned to hear the new supreme commander, as he strode back and forth across the floor in energetic pacing, castigate the air force crews under Brett's command. He manifested little more than "contempt and criticism for them" and, Brett added later,[21] said that they lacked "discipline, organization, purposeful intent."

(Some months later, when General George C. Kenney replaced Brett—one of the direct results of the survey mission—General Kenney received the same criticism of the air forces. Because it is germane to the subject, it is worth noting that Kenney was to quote MacArthur as saying that the air forces were "an inefficient rabble of boulevard shock troops." MacArthur added that not only were the airmen antagonistic to him and to his headquarters, but through this antagonism they had reached the "point of disloyalty." Another diatribe was delivered to General Kenney by Lieutenant General Richard K. Sutherland, MacArthur's chief of staff, who railed against Brett in particular, questioned the courage of the men flying against the Japanese, and then alienated himself from the Australians forever when they learned that he described the Aussies as "undisciplined, untrained, over-advertised and generally useless . . .")

This, then, was the high-echelon background to the war in the Southwest Pacific; the setting for the stage upon which Lyndon Johnson was about to make an entrance.

CHAPTER THREE

MEETING EN ROUTE

Of all the people that Lyndon Johnson met and worked with during his mission for President Roosevelt, no one affected his schedules, itinerary, and activities more than Lieutenant Colonel Samuel E. Anderson.* Anderson, a professional career soldier and airman, and Johnson were to establish a relationship that through meetings, contacts, and mutual projects has endured since those days in the Pacific.† The role that Sam Anderson and, for a period almost as great in the

* Retired from active duty, United States Air Force, with four-star rank, on January 31, 1963.

† AAF officers who were with Anderson and Johnson during their tour of the SWPA noted that Anderson at that time—and he has ever since—was one of the few men who ever addressed Lyndon Johnson simply as "Johnnie."

Pacific area, Lieutenant Colonel Francis R. Stevens played in the future of Lyndon Johnson was to be profound indeed.

Early in 1942, Colonel Anderson was serving with the Operations and Plans Division (OPD) of the War Department General Staff in Washington. As a member of the General Staff, Anderson participated actively in the plans for implementing the nation's capacity to combat the enemy in all global theaters. The OPD itself was divided into geographic sections; Colonel Anderson personally was responsible for air-planning activities in the Southwest Pacific Area (SWPA). Because of this background and Anderson's extensive experience as a military officer, as well as because of his reputation for brilliance in planning, he proved to be an ideal associate for Lieutenant Commander Johnson during the survey.

The situation in the SWPA early in 1942 "looked very grim," Anderson noted. But he added the cautious observation that the *manner* in which the situation could be judged depended entirely upon one's geographical location.

"Viewpoints of the same conditions can be grossly different," Anderson emphasized. "Back in the States we were tremendously worried about the scarcity of forces and the problems of supplying these forces—setting up a proper chain of command, just to begin with. We knew there were two specific and immediate objectives. The first was to stop the Japanese advance from penetrating more deeply into the southwest Pacific, and, second, just turn that advance in such a direction that, when it finally did come to a halt, conditions would allow us better to pick the time and the place to begin the countermoves along the road that ultimately would allow us to destroy the war machine of the Japanese." [22]

Lieutenant Colonel Stevens also toured the SWPA with Lyndon Johnson. He, too, was from the General Staff in Washington and had worked extensively with Anderson. The two General Staff officers met Lyndon Johnson entirely by chance in Nouméa, New Caledonia. But that accidental meeting grew into sound professional and personal relationships during the weeks of intensive trips, dozens of flights and survey tasks, the comparing of notes, and discussions long into the night—all activities that might be expected of three men, each of whom had individually been selected for his exceptional abilities.

At first, Commander Johnson knew little about the field conditions of military forces. Yet his congressional experience on military affairs committees stood him in good stead and, as events proved clearly, he soon perceived the true nature of conditions and problems in the SWPA. Anderson and many other officers who kept good records at that time noted that "he was a man very quick to learn, to take full advantage of the experience and the assistance of others with more experience particularly in these fields; thus armed with this shared experience, he attended to his own investigations with remarkable efficiency."

It was Anderson who, as an officer well versed in air warfare, noted to Johnson that what appeared as a clear and unblemished color in Washington assumed an altogether different hue "when you saw it from the immediate proximity of the combat theater."

Anderson explained that "when you got out into the field, you learned quickly that although those people out there had the same problems you had always known about, there was a critical difference to be considered. A problem read in a report is entirely different when the problem is one demanding personal attention and solution. Those people had critical problems of getting the gasoline they needed so badly just to keep their planes in the air. They had to scream and beg and even borrow (from the Australians) the bombs and ammunition they needed to fight the war. Feeding the men was a constant, aggravating problem. They didn't even have the clothes they needed for everyday wear! Reading about a shortage of shoes when you're in Washington, and walking barefoot on a hot desert, may be the same problem, but it's a long way different in its individual meaning. The people in the SWPA were at the real end of the line at that time, and it was rough going for them."

Anderson's comments are particularly germane to this story. They reflect, first, the situation as seen through the eyes of the man that Generals H. H. Arnold and E. Hull considered to be one of the best-qualified military observers in all of Washington. They are his observations, stripped bare of the ponderous notations and cross-references of archives and presented unencumbered in form. And they are, finally, a clear representation of what was seen, experienced, and judged by the naval officer who, some twenty-two years later, was to become the President of the United States.

"There was particular concern," Anderson has explained, "with the situation in the air. The Japanese had exploited their airpower in a fashion that left little argument as to its effectiveness; after all, we *were* pretty tired of being pushed back so far and for so long. Air was the key to the southwest Pacific, and we had precious little to bring to bear against the Japanese. The lines of communication even within that theater were tremendous. Few people realize that Australia itself is almost as large as the entire continental United States. The distance from Melbourne—where MacArthur had his headquarters—up to New Guinea, where the actual fighting was going on, was a matter of some fifteen hundred miles. Communications were worse than poor. Compared to what we considered even basic communications, they might even be described as wretched.

"General MacArthur didn't arrive in Australia until the 18th of March, and then he moved south to set up his headquarters in Melbourne. Although he was commanding all the air forces and wanted to move closer to the area of operations, General Brett as MacArthur's top staff officer had no choice but to remain close to the supreme commander of Allied Forces. They had to work together, of course, but this didn't help the combat situation when the few fighting forces were scraping themselves raw so very much farther to the north. The most active bomb groups—and especially the 22d, which had been told to go out and win air superiority from the Japanese—were based in the vicinity of Townsville in the northeastern part of the continent. Melbourne, however, lies at the extreme southeastern tip, and a really personal command from higher headquarters was an impossibility at that time."

The decision to send Colonels Anderson and Stevens, representing the air and ground forces, to Australia to meet MacArthur shortly after his arrival was to serve two purposes. Both men would establish clearly the desire of General Staff officers to maintain a close relationship with MacArthur. At the same time, they would obtain MacArthur's own evaluation of conditions in the SWPA—and in the supreme commander's own words. Despite the fact that Anderson was "air" and Stevens was "ground," both men had long worked closely together in OPD, sharing their assignment to the Southwest Pacific. The decision to send them to Australia to confer with MacArthur was made on the basis of a critical need to obtain an objective analysis of the situation; the time between their being notified of their orders and their departure from Washington was less than eighteen hours.

There followed a commercial flight from Washington on May 4, 1942, to San Francisco (arrival on the fifth). Exactly at midnight on May 6,[23] the two men departed the United States in a new Boeing B-17E Flying Fortress (destined for the 19th Bomb Group in Australia). Anderson was hardly a passenger, since he had also been assigned the mission of flying the trip as copilot. For the next three days they worked their way from San Francisco across the Pacific via Hawaii, Christmas Island, Canton Island, the Fiji Islands, and finally Nouméa, New Caledonia.

There they were stranded. They arrived immediately after the end of the Battle of the Coral Sea, and even while both sides debated among themselves as to who the victor was in that engagement, another huge conflict between American and Japanese naval forces was shaping up (this became the

Battle of Midway). Everyone on New Caledonia seemed to be convinced that a full-scale invasion of the island by the Japanese was imminent, and defensive preparations to repel the attack were under way around the clock. Every available aircraft was being thrown into bombed-up patrol duty to seek out the Japanese fleet. With a spanking-new B-17E available to him, the American commander on New Caledonia was not about to let the airplane slip out of his hands, and it was immediately taken away from Anderson and Stevens.

Although the orders for the two officers instructed them to "proceed with the greatest possible speed" to MacArthur's headquarters in Melbourne, the two men had no choice but to spend the next eight days in New Caledonia, trying vainly to find some means of transportation to leave the island. All aircraft, however, were coming north to the New Caledonia area, and none were being allowed to depart, so severe was the shortage of combat planes. This delay in the departure of Anderson and Stevens brought about their fateful meeting with Lyndon Johnson.

On May 21, a huge Consolidated PB2Y-2 Coronado flying boat roared in from the east for a landing in the harbor. Anderson and Stevens, who had received word the day before of the expected arrival of the plane, eyed the flying boat anxiously; it just might be able to carry them on their way. The Coronado turned out to be the personal transport of Vice Admiral Robert L. Ghormley, arriving in the area to take up his new command of the South Pacific Force and Area. Ghormley was then under the orders of Admiral Ernest J. King to "establish your headquarters in Auckland with an advanced base at Tongatapu." ‡

Aboard Ghormley's flying boat, en route to MacArthur's headquarters to begin his mission, was Lyndon Johnson. Prior to leaving the United States, Johnson had been given the opportunity to observe closely the activities and planning of Admiral Ghormley and his staff. It had been a hectic time, for Ghormley had arrived in Washington, after a hasty trip from London, England, as late as April 17. Immediately upon deplaning in Washington, the admiral had been thrown directly into the responsibilities of his new post. Ghormley was in the

‡ The noted naval historian, Samuel Eliot Morison, in his *History of United States Naval Operations in World War II*, Vol. IV: *Coral Sea, Midway and Submarine Actions*, states on p. 253 that "Ghormley arrived at Nouméa 17 May . . ." This date is in dispute, for Sam Anderson's flight log lists the date of Ghormley's arrival as May 21. The War History Branch of the New Zealand government (see note 5) states that Ghormley arrived in Auckland on May 21, Pacific Time (May 22, Washington Time). Anderson's flight-log record of a departure from Nouméa on May 21, with arrival in Auckland on May 22, is unquestionably accurate.

position of being the man to begin the first phase of sustained naval operations against the Japanese, driving northward from the South Pacific. He was to spend until the fall of 1942 preparing and planning for the long drive toward the Japanese homeland; no one had any doubts but that it would take monumental effort to build up the military force that would be required to make even the first steps in this long-range plan. No help at all could be found in the knowledge that, despite the critical nature of the situation throughout the Pacific, Washington had decided that the press of the war against Germany had to keep supplies to the Pacific on a "limited deployment."

During several weeks spent in Washington, Ghormley hand-picked a staff of some forty officers. By May 1, he was winging his way across the Pacific, bound for Pearl Harbor, with Commander Johnson a passenger in the Coronado flying boat. Ghormley remained at Pearl for a week in order to hold conferences with Admiral Nimitz and his staff. It was an unusual opportunity for all concerned to study in detail the strength, plans, and action in the Pacific, for while Nimitz and Ghormley mapped out future campaigns, the Battle of the Coral Sea was taking place. The men learned at the time that, while there existed grave doubts as to an American naval victory, at the least the United States Navy had stopped a major Japanese thrust to invade and occupy the critical area of Port Moresby on New Guinea's southeastern coast.

It was also to prove a dramatic lesson in the realities of combat—as the men assembled with Admiral Nimitz learned —compared to what the American people received at home. Historians have listed the Battle of the Coral Sea as a "tactical victory" for the Japanese, but a "failure" in the strategic sense. It is argued that the two Japanese carriers that suffered damage in the air strikes made by our planes were unable to participate in the impending Battle of Midway (in which the Japanese Navy suffered a calamitous defeat), when their participation might well have tipped the scales in Japan's favor. Whatever the "if" of such speculation, there was no question but that the "true" and "public" stories of the Battle of the Coral Sea were miles apart.

In addition to two other ships, the United States lost the big aircraft carrier *Lexington*—a loss that we could ill afford at that time. The *only* major Japanese warship to go to the bottom was the light carrier *Shoho*.

The *New York Times* announced the battle in front-page streamer headlines:

JAPANESE REPULSED IN GREAT PACIFIC BATTLE WITH 17 TO 22 OF THEIR SHIPS SUNK OR CRIPPLED; ENEMY IN FLIGHT, PURSUED BY ALLIED WARSHIPS.

When the Coronado flying boat arrived on May 21 in

Nouméa harbor, several members of Ghormley's staff left the airplane to set up field headquarters for Ghormley on New Caledonia proper. The crew refueled the plane and prepared for a take-off as quickly as was possible—but not before Anderson and Stevens "managed to beg a ride with Admiral Ghormley."

It was at this point that they met Commander Johnson, who, Anderson later recalled, was "tall, thin, good-looking, very energetic. He impressed you with his clear and precise speech which, even though he sometimes spoke quite rapidly, was unusually articulate."

Neither Anderson nor Stevens had any idea that Johnson was other than what he seemed to be: "just another member of Admiral Ghormley's staff. I didn't have any idea at all," Anderson related, "and found out only later that this lieutenant commander was actually a Congressman, and also a representative of President Roosevelt, and he was en route to Australia to conduct much the same kind of mission for the President that Stevens and I were doing for the War Department General Staff. We didn't know this at the time, and we learned that few people, if there was anyone besides Admiral Ghormley, knew about Johnson's true status. He just kept it to himself.

"We were grateful when Admiral Ghormley very kindly took Stevens and myself on board. On the 21st of May we took off from Nouméa in the flying boat and flew directly to Auckland, New Zealand, where the admiral was to establish his new headquarters."

That night, Anderson, Stevens, and Johnson stayed at the same hotel in Auckland. It was after dinner that they had their first opportunity to get to know one another. The three men "were sitting in the lobby, relaxing, talking to one another. During our conversation we learned—it just seemed to come out in the talking, when we brought up our missions—that Johnson was on his special mission for the President, and that he, too, was en route to Melbourne to see MacArthur. The more we talked things over, the more we were all struck with the realization that our missions were almost identical. We were all three searching for the same information; the only difference was that we were to report our findings to different superiors.

"It was right then and there that the three of us made our agreement that, since we were all looking for the same information, we would stick close together throughout our time in the southwest Pacific. We agreed to carry out our assignments together, almost as a team. From the moment that we had the opportunity to discuss at length what we were all after, we found Commander Johnson to be a warm and friendly individual. The President—in my opinion, and this was shared as well by Stevens—could not have picked a sharper man than Johnson for the task he had been given. The speed with which he gained comprehension of the difficult matters in the theater was remarkable, and a pleasure to witness."

It should be made clear that all three officers, despite their association with different elements of the armed services, in terms of land, sea, and air, had assignments to study the general situation rather than any one particular area or phase of operations.

"Commander Johnson was interested in the over-all problem of what our combat forces were trying to overcome in the southwest Pacific," Anderson related. "He was out to pinpoint and to try to understand the nature of their difficulties. His mission—and this was absolutely clear—was to be able to return to the President with the kind of information he needed to cut through conflicting reports from the SWPA, and to carry out his planning with a clearly objective analysis of the situation in that theater."

Johnson's meeting with Anderson and Stevens turned out to be fortuitous indeed. He had already completed the major part of his journey across the Pacific when he met them. Quite suddenly he was in the company of two highly skilled officers whose knowledge and experience could and did help to bridge whatever gaps existed in Johnson's own grasp of the subject he had come to the Pacific to survey.

Sam Anderson noted carefully Johnson's ability "to assess an over-all situation—he was extremely sharp in everything I ever saw him do—but at the same time our viewpoints and experience certainly couldn't hurt. Perhaps our ideas and our convictions, and our own observations as well, proved of assistance to Johnson. I don't know and can only surmise this.

"But there is one thing I wish to make absolutely clear for the record: Commander Johnson was interested in, and he was determined to see, things for himself. Any tendency by anyone to emphasize that Stevens was a ground-forces officer, that I was an airman, and Johnson a naval officer simply didn't carry any importance worth mentioning. All three of us were interested in the general, the over-all, situation as it affected all the military forces. The uniforms that we wore, reflecting our service backgrounds, did little else than that—they had no place in affecting the tasks we had individually, and collectively, of course, set out to perform."

On the morning of May 23 the PB2Y-2 carried the three officers to Sydney, Australia. This was to be the last leg of their journey in the Coronado. The flying boat was big, and for more than ten hours it lumbered through the skies. The four propellers battered the slabsided fuselage with an avalanche of noise, and passengers of the airplane remember its ability to sap the strength of a man through the constant hammering din and the vibration. But it had not been built for comfort—it was a patrol bomber.

The long trek across the ocean gave the three men a chance to discuss at some length "what we wanted to do in Australia, other than going through the motions of simply reporting to General MacArthur. None of us wanted any 'set' or 'carefully planned' itinerary that would show us a limited or 'favored' view of the situation. So while we had the opportunity, we went over the matter of what we would do when we reached Australia. We already knew certain areas where we would encounter the kind of problems that were causing local anguish that echoed all the way back to Washington—the worst of which was communications. We wanted to be certain we could get to the worst of the problem areas ourselves, and not have to take anyone's word—beyond the basic briefings—for anything.

"Before we landed we agreed to make a tour of every installation in the Southwest Pacific Area that we could possibly reach. This included, as well, the huge and still growing training installations around Melbourne proper. Because American soldiers were being trained by the Aussies, we wanted a good look at that situation."

It was a long and tiring flight. In between the several discussions they had, Johnson went through his papers and notes, moved throughout the aircraft, or simply rested. Anderson and Stevens tried to while away the time playing cribbage.

They arrived on the night of the twenty-third in Sydney and checked in as quickly as possible at the Australia House. They were all so bone-weary that they agreed to an early dinner, and retired almost immediately afterward.

On the morning of May 24, they found that the idea of getting military transportation to fly them southward to Melbourne along the coast was nothing more than a hope. Aircraft were so scarce that not a plane was available to transport them to MacArthur's headquarters. Wasting no time, they managed to get aboard a small Australian commercial airliner. The Lockheed 12 § twin-engined transport carried them southward to Melbourne in a slow and uneventful flight, landing in the late afternoon. By the time they checked into the Menzies Hotel, it was already evening. Although General MacArthur was quartered in the same hotel, the visiting trio deferred their first meeting until the following morning.

Early on May 25, Johnson, Anderson, and Stevens were

§ The same basic design as the Lockheed transport flown by Amelia Earhart on her final and fatal Pacific flight.

ushered into the office of MacArthur's chief of staff, General Sutherland.|| Their meeting was more introductory than anything else, and after a "few minutes with Sutherland," they were taken directly into General MacArthur's office.

They walked into a large, well-furnished room. At the far end, MacArthur waited for them behind a large desk. After their greeting, the general indicated they were to be seated in "very comfortable lounge chairs."

Then, for almost an hour, the supreme commander strode up and down the part of the room behind his desk. The meeting contained little in the way of conversation. Instead, the hour consisted of, as Anderson later recalled, "mostly a monologue delivered by General MacArthur."

The three visitors then explained their mission and detailed their intentions to the general. They were delighted to find that, instead of attempting to force upon them an itinerary prepared by his staff, MacArthur offered his assistance "in whatever you need to carry out your responsibilities, and to fulfill your mission." At their request, General MacArthur then outlined for them a plan of inspection and a general itinerary—one that would give them the maximum amount of leeway.

Following an inspection of the major industrial and training sites in the immediate vicinity, they were to begin a trip that "would send us up the east coast and on into New Guinea, across to Darwin in northwest Australia, and finally back to Melbourne, during which time we would visit as many air, ground, and navy installations as it was possible to do," related Anderson.

General MacArthur "took special pains" to emphasize to his visitors that shortcomings in communications in his theater were so critical as to be seriously undermining his effort to combat the Japanese. The general painted a picture that "could hardly be considered as encouraging," and yet, Anderson noted at the time, "he sounds determined, very determined." Looking back on that visit with MacArthur in Melbourne, Anderson added the observation that the "whole session was what you might call a 'tour de force,' such as only General MacArthur could do."

Anderson, Stevens, and Johnson agreed among themselves that until their meeting with MacArthur they had not received a "true, up-to-date assessment of the situation as it really exists in the southwest Pacific." They were pleased by the candor of the supreme commander during his meeting with them—something that could not have been truly predicted.

Immediately after the three men took leave of MacArthur,

|| A man about whom General George C. Kenney has said: ". . . an unfortunate bit of arrogance combined with his egotism had made him almost universally disliked."

the general's staff—under his orders to simply display every aspect of the picture as it existed, and to answer whatever questions were put to them—prepared a series of thorough intelligence, operations, and communications briefings. Looked at in the cold light of the facts and figures as presented to the three officers from Washington, the situation grimly underscored the persistent fears of an invasion of the Japanese against Australia proper.

With the briefing sessions in MacArthur's headquarters completed, Anderson excused himself and hurried over to the headquarters of General Brett. As the personal emissary of General H. H. Arnold, Anderson requested and received "absolutely complete and thorough briefings from Brett's corresponding operations: intelligence, communications, and plans." For there was something to be gleaned from the AAF briefing that could not be obtained elsewhere, and it had nothing to do with frankness and honesty; rather, it was a matter of attitudes. The AAF was carrying the brunt of the war in the SWPA, and the man who is personally bearing the load is always more sensitive to the problems of the task than anyone else could be.

There remained one final session with MacArthur before the three officers were ready to take their leave. The general reiterated that he agreed fully with the three observers from Washington as to their stated requirements; he made much of his own point of view that the only way to taste the true situation was to get out into the field, as, indeed, they planned to do.

He rose to his feet and looked at them. "When you have done all this, when you have completed your inspections," he said, "come back here and see me."

The determination of Douglas MacArthur, the three men noted to themselves, did not transfer itself to his staff, and they spoke among themselves of the fact that "most of the briefings were pretty gloomy."

Once again, Anderson noted, communications was the greatest weakness. "This in particular was very bad," he explained, "even worse, much worse, than we had feared. With the Japanese grinding their way south, MacArthur's own intelligence people simply could not be optimistic. There had been disturbing talk of Australia's being abandoned, talk that shook up the Australians and brought vehement denials of any such contemplation on the part of the United States government.

"No one in Australia ever considered *abandoning* the country to the Japanese, but at the same time they had no possible opportunity to plan anything of a measurable scale against the enemy, and that was a terribly frustrating thing to live with. The only real fighting MacArthur's staff at Melbourne could even consider was the matter of long-range planning, all of it waiting to be done *when,* and *if,* they ever got the forces required to carry out their hopes."

Johnson, Anderson and Stevens were ready to find out about that "when" and "if."

CHAPTER FOUR

THIS WAS AUSTRALIA

As Johnson, Anderson, and Stevens walked from the entrance of MacArthur's headquarters, they discussed the itinerary they would pursue during the immediate weeks ahead. The schedule as recommended by a MacArthur staff officer included firsthand surveys of the main training centers and facilities in the country lying just outside Melbourne; each night the three men would return to the Menzies Hotel. They planned to spend only two or three days at this activity and then depart for bases much farther to the north—the bases from which missions were being flown against the Japanese in their conquered bases on New Guinea, New Britain, Portuguese Timor, and elsewhere.

As might be expected, conditions were such that any hope for a definite schedule of movement was soon abandoned. The trio was to fly northward in a battered old B-17D bomber known as "The Swoose," which was General Brett's personal aircraft, flown by Major Frank Kurtz and so old and weary that it was employed for transportation rather than for combat.* The early-model Flying Fortress, however, was grounded because of the lack of spare parts and would be unable to become airborne until her mechanics scrounged and improvised the materials needed for repairs.

If any of the three officers on their inspection mission wanted immediate proof of the supply problem, they had it almost at once. They were stuck in Melbourne until transportation was available for them.

The lack of such transportation permitted a "more exten-

---

* Captain Colin Kelly, Jr., America's first World War II hero, was flying a B-17D on December 10, 1941, when he was shot down near Clark Field in the Philippines. The same Frank Kurtz who flew "The Swoose" for General Brett, on December 10 was in the Clark Field control tower at the time and watched the body of his close friend Kelly strike the ground about two hundred yards from the spot where his flaming bomber crashed and exploded.

sive than planned" study by Johnson, Anderson, and Stevens of the training and cantonment areas around Melbourne. The three observers were both surprised at and delighted with one camp in particular. Here, they discovered, most of the first American troops to arrive in Australia were busily undergoing training for jungle and desert warfare and for combinations of everything in between. The majority of instructors, noted the Washington observers, were hardened Australian veterans who had fought both the Germans in the African desert and the Japanese invaders to the north of Australia. Anderson at this time made special note for the report he was preparing that the Australians were "rough, hardened, and no-nonsense combat veterans who have learned the truth of kill or be killed; not a doubt about that. They are giving our people the best training there is available."

The three Washington observers ultimately visited every camp and training installation in the area. With them was a small escort group assigned to their party by General MacArthur. The supreme commander insisted that his entire staff be fully aware of his desire that *Congressman*—not Lieutenant Commander—Johnson be accorded VIP treatment. Johnson, who had taken pains on many occasions to represent himself only as a naval officer on a survey mission, did not appear overly happy with MacArthur's deferential treatment, but there was little he could do about it. One example of the VIP status assigned to Johnson and the two General Staff officers of lieutenant-colonel rank was the presence of William F. Marquat, a brigadier general (antiaircraft artillery) assigned to escort three officers of considerably subordinate rank.

There was very little in the way of aerial-combat forces or installations to see in Melbourne. Anderson explained that there was "one commercial airfield where there were a few old training aircraft, some decrepit old commercial planes, and the battered and unfortunately grounded old Swoose. It wasn't much of a field by anyone's standards, and it would have been a crime even to have considered it as a military installation."

There was to be demonstrated still another lesson on life in Australia that involved the strictest possible military censorship on the part of American and Australian authorities—but that did not have a thing to do with military security. Anderson and Stevens were well acquainted with the policy of news suppression, military or otherwise, when the release of such information might "rock the boat" of command which high-level officers desired to keep nice and steady. As a Congressman agile in the no-holds-barred world of American politics, Johnson could hardly have been surprised by such practices, and might have been even more surprised had he found them absent.

However, in Australia, Lyndon Johnson ran into a situation

involving American troops that he might well have expected to find in the United States, especially in the South, but which presented an unexpected and unusually serious problem in Australia. It was a situation that involved prejudice and segregation of American Negro soldiers, *and even their exclusion from Australia, as requested by the Australian government.*

Had this occurred in peacetime, it would have been an unpleasant problem, demanding solution, though the answer might be wanting or even considerably delayed, but still a matter to be resolved on a stage with familiar backdrops and surroundings.

Australia in late May of 1942 did not present a normal scene. It was a world in which disaster hung menacingly over the entire northern horizon—a world in which American, Australian, British, French, Dutch, Philippine, Chinese, and other combat forces had been pounded and whipped almost at will by the steamrolling Japanese war machine. Those same Japanese were tearing apart Darwin and at the same time building up a great invasion force with which, intelligence reported, they intended to assault Australia proper. There were rumors and counterrumors of Australia's being abandoned because it was indefensible. The existence of the nation was at stake, and those men who knew of the behavior of Japanese Army troops with prisoners and civilians looked ahead to the coming months with fear in their hearts.

Under these frightening circumstances, the Australian government still hewed to ". . . the maintenance of a 'white Australia.'" Despite all the foregoing that had to be considered, the elements of government in Australia still placed this white-supremacy policy on a level of greater urgency than the threatened invasion of the continent! "The establishment of barriers against the immigration of black, brown, and yellow races has received the support of all political parties, and could not be ignored by American military authorities." [24]

Incredible as all this might seem, even as Japanese bombs smashed into Darwin and killed hundreds of Australian citizens, the Australian government was so adamant on the matter that its protestations about American Negro troops' being shipped to Australia to defend that country jarred the highest official levels of Washington, D.C.

Official documents note that

". . . two colored units were scheduled to sail: Company G and Company L of the 31st QM Regiment (Truck). When Australia's 'white' policy was called to the attention of A-3 † at Headquarters in Washington, orders for the movement of these two companies were cancelled and orders were issued

† Operations.

for the . . . only white quartermaster truck companies then available to the Air Force Combat Command.

". . . the War Plans Division had previously directed that no colored troops should be sent to Australia for a permanent change of station, inasmuch as the Australian government had expressed an unfavorable attitude when the question was raised. The urgent need for labor battalions in Australia, though, soon caused that government to ease its restrictions and allow the entrance of colored troops, *with the understanding that they were to be withdrawn when they were no longer needed.*" [25] [Italics added.]

Things went from bad to worse in the matter. The uproar so effectively concealed from the public through strict military censorship finally reached such proportions that President Roosevelt was prevailed upon specifically to render a judgment of national policy in the matter.

(A memorandum for the Chief of Staff by A-3, dated January 16, 1942, indicates beyond any question whatsoever the serious nature of the conflict within military echelons. This memo stressed that, "in addition to the situation in Australia, the State Department has directed that no colored troops be sent to Panama or Liberia for a permanent change of station." A-3 officers became so angered over State Department orders for such segregation that they demanded that the question be submitted directly to the President for a decision, since it appeared that "white troops would be sent out of the United States to foreign stations and that the colored troops would remain in the United States for the defense of the country. It is believed that this is neither the intention nor the spirit of the Promulgation of the President in this period of an unlimited National Emergency.")

What compounded the confusion already existing in the matter was the huge gulf that clearly existed between the policy of the Australian government and the actions of the Australian people. These wonderful people, grateful for their chance to survive the Japanese invasion they deemed inevitable, apparently could not have cared less about the color of skin of the American soldiers, and no incidents or disturbances between the Australian people and American Negro troops are to be found in the official archives.

Yet the issue persisted. President Roosevelt, already annoyed with the vexing problem, found it lying once more at his doorstep when new reports coming in from Australia noted carefully that "the principal clashes in Australia occurred not between the Australians and the colored, but between the American white and colored troops. The situation was such that General Brett, on 25 March, recommended the withdrawal of all colored troops" from Australia.[26] (That recommendation was speedily and angrily rejected by Washington.)

It was impossible for Johnson, Anderson, and Stevens to avoid this subject, even though there was on the part of the MacArthur command staff an "obvious reluctance to openly discuss the matter," Anderson noted. He and Stevens as part of the General Staff had available to them the documents reporting on the situation in Australia, and as the personal representative of President Roosevelt in the SWPA, Johnson had the obligation to survey the "entire general situation."

The conflict of American policy versus Australian policy concerning Negro troops was an aggravating burr in Washington that refused simply to go away. Shortly before the departure of Anderson and Stevens from Washington, further reports were prepared for the perusal of the General Staff in the form of a memorandum, Number 300.6, from the Air Adjutant General's office, and dated April 4, 1942. That the situation was considered far from closed is evident in the actions of the General Staff when a full statement of the War Department Policy was made pertaining, in the spring of 1942, to the use of Negro troops in different theaters of operations; this statement was established as a further guide line for the various military agencies. The official policy was contained in a letter from the Adjutant General to the Commanding General, Army Air Forces, May 13, 1942, and was filed permanently in the office of the Air Adjutant General, AAG 381 F, War Plans. This latter communication was prepared even while Anderson, Johnson, and Stevens were en route to Australia.

While not pressing the subject with MacArthur's staff, Anderson did not ignore the matter; he was by no means complacent about such an explosive issue. Associates of Anderson describe him as a "sharp-eyed observer with a memory for detail that can only be described as astounding." With full knowledge of the secret reports sent to Washington on the incidents in Australia, and aware of the dogged insistence of the Australian government on sustaining its "white supremacy" policies in the face of possible military disaster, Anderson took every opportunity to ascertain through his own observations and experiences the exact nature of the situation.

"What I saw down there was the exact opposite of the reports that had reached the General Staff in Washington," he commented. "Were we to believe some of the statements of the officials of the Australian government, the presence of American Negro troops would precipitate major crises and fatal riots in Australia.

"Well, when the colored troops arrived there, nothing of the sort happened. There was a complete acceptance of our soldiers, colored or white, by the Australian people. I made it a point to watch for this carefully. I saw Australian families take Negro troops to church, and bring them from the church into their homes as their guests. I never saw a single case of unpleasantness, or aversion, or hostility, of any kind, on the part of the Australian people.

"As a matter of fact, we considered this matter so important that I included a long section on my observations. I gave the conclusion that the American Negro troops seemed to be accepted completely and without reservation by the Australian population."

Long before Johnson, Anderson, and Stevens left the United States for Australia, they were aware of the tremendous problem of getting combat supplies to both our Allies and our own forces in the distant Southwest Pacific Area (SWPA). Direct transport to places almost halfway around the globe was not possible because of the dominion of Japanese influence and the reach of Japanese submarines; individual ships as well as convoys were slowed down by the necessity of taking erratic paths across the ocean. Those vessels that, despite enemy action, did finally make it to Australia, with her ports being bombed and the Japanese pushing ever closer in the north, were of value beyond all measurement. The weapons and supplies delivered to the Australians and the Americans who were carrying the battle were making the difference between survival and defeat. Certainly, if the supply lines were severed and supplies were cut off, it would be only a matter of time before the Japanese swept over the opposition.

In a time of emergency, speed in unloading vessels can always be assured simply by adopting emergency measures, by dismissing all considerations other than those necessary to get the job done. In this case, time was a critical factor in getting and keeping the combat forces supplied and in action against the enemy. Civilian labor—especially stevedores—held the key to such speed in unloading the precious combat supplies from newly arrived merchantmen.

Lyndon Johnson had long been a friend of labor. He prided himself on this relationship and on the things he had done to benefit the workingman. He was also a realist and, as he had on many occasions told the American worker, there were moments of national emergency when personal benefits and advantages had to be laid aside for the common good. We faced in early 1942 what Johnson and many others recognized as nothing less than a dire emergency. Johnson had warned again and again that the likelihood of America's being involved in war became greater with every passing month. He had stressed that it was necessary to yield, temporarily, personal advantages in order to help strengthen the nation during a national emergency—because an outbreak of war threatened the very existence of the nation and all its workers.

Consider, once again, the situation in May of 1942 when Johnson arrived in Australia. Consider the weakness of our own forces after six months of devastating defeat at the hands of the Japanese. Mark well the ever-present threat of Japanese invasion, the spread of rumor that Australia might be abandoned.

At the time that these conditions existed, elements of Australian labor—notably many of the men who worked on the docks unloading munitions and supply ships from the United States—completely ignored the Japanese threat to their island homeland and, come what may, refused to yield an inch in any of their "contract rights." On a number of occasions they interfered seriously with American attempts to aid Australia.

In sum, equipment desperately needed by our combat forces was being held up for inordinately long and exasperating periods of time, and the men who were fighting with jury-rigged equipment on the combat front were described as "white with anger" when reports of activities in Australian ports reached them.

"The task of unloading . . . equipment was frequently a source of dismay to the Americans, who could not reconcile with the pressure of the war the terms under which Australian stevedores worked. According to Major Earl C. Stewart, assistant military attaché at Melbourne, the stevedores worked under iron-clad contracts which were drawn up solely in the interest of the laborers, who in turn paid little attention to the actual number of hours they were scheduled to work. . . . *The contract stipulation that the men should not work in the rain usually resulted in the cessation of work at the first drop of rain. The suspension of cargo handling on all holidays and weekends was also an inviolable rule.* [Italics added.]

"To the Air Corps men who were anxiously awaiting the unloading of their crated planes and equipment, this situation was beyond comprehension. On a few occasions, when a particularly critical cargo was to be unloaded, American troops were used; *but this practice was never made general, since it might have precipitated a crisis.*" [29] [Italics added.]

The feelings of the Americans—described officially as "beyond comprehension"—obviously were fanned to a white heat. The situation then existing in the SWPA can be evaluated only in the light of knowledge of what American ground crewmen were being forced to endure as they worked frantically to carry on the fight against the Japanese.

Compare the preceding official report of the situation at

Australian ports and the conduct of the Australian stevedores with the following excerpt from the records of an American fighter squadron, contained in official-history material:

"Our camp area was located about a mile from the airfield, next to a creek, with mud and tall grass all around and millions of mosquitos. The men were not allowed to set up tents due to the threat of a Jap invasion. The tents were tan colored and were not easily camouflaged, so they strung shelter halves over their cots to keep off the rain. During the first three weeks at Tantouta, the men were working 24 hours a day assembling planes and morale went to a very low degree.

"It rained so much that everyone's bed and personal belongings were always wet. The mosquitos were so thick that men nearly went crazy trying to keep them away. They got in the food, inside mosquito netting, and settled down on anything and everything that even looked human. Quite a few of the men became sick with fatigue and diarrhea but even with all the hardships we had to put up with, the squadron assembled 25 airplanes in 19 days. . . .

"The clothing and bedding constantly became soaked, mildewed, fly-blown and ruined. Many nights were spent in soaked clothes under sopping blankets while rain dripped through the shelter halves and trickled in rivulets underneath. Trucks churned the camp site into a mush of miasmic mud.

"But the most agonizing were the mosquitos—the damned mosquitos. They were so thick, one swipe of the hand over any part of the body could be made to kill at least three. Customary dress was a headnet to protect the face and neck, gloves for the hands, and boots or trousers tucked into the heavy sox for the ankles. But they bit through shirts and pants and switches of tree leaves were used to slap them off the back. When they got under the headnet you were really busy.

"Several men in nearby outfits went out of their heads due to the intolerable, agonizing worry from the stinging and had to be hospitalized. Then there was the long epidemic of diarrhea and cramps which caused suffering and enervation of much of the personnel. A wad of paper—for emergency use—was carried at all times. The combination of diarrhea and mosquitos was intolerable, since the former made tender parts of the body especially vulnerable, many times a day, to the latter. . . ."

Here are some notes penciled by a veteran Army master sergeant Robert Foye, who was line chief during this period:

"No replacement parts. Every fifth crate was designated 'spare parts' before it was uncrated. . . .

"Rain, mud, and mosquitos. Mechanics worked sopping wet. Pvt. Jones worked on tail assembly sitting in six inches of water, so wet from rain he never knew the difference. Rain poured down their faces and necks—still they worked on, passing the scanty wrenches from one to another. Not a growl from any man. . . .

"Mechanics became production-conscious and still section chiefs would urge them on. Assembly ran like a factory—all in the open and all in the mud. Would put any depot to shame . . . Every man to his job, and never a growl except when one section chief would hold up another: 'Come on! this is war. Keep 'em rolling.' . . .

"During the second week of assembly, officers and men began to come down with dysentery. Men literally dropped on their knees with cramps at the rig before they would ask for relief. Had to be ordered home, sometimes even threatened with trial for disobedience of orders for refusing to leave their place on the line. Why hasn't Washington designed a decoration for men in the Air Corps who, far above and beyond the call of duty, perform feats on the ground? . . .

"It would be impossible to pick out outstanding men during this period—when they worked from 5 A.M. until dark in the mud and rain and then volunteered to go back at night. The whole outfit was outstanding. An outfit like this could be the nucleus for six Air Corps groups and with recruit fill-ins could start operating tomorrow. . . .

"Such was the rush [continues the official report] that on two nights they rigged up field floodlights for an attempt at 24-hour assembly. But mosquitos were driving the men insane and it had to be stopped. Once there was an air raid scare and pilots and men spent all night dragging uncrated planes around with trucks to dispersal points. . . ." [30]

Meanwhile, on the docks, Australian stevedores immediately ended their work "at the first drop of rain" and religiously observed the sacred rule of never handling cargo on "all holidays and weekends"!

Were Johnson, Anderson, and Stevens aware of these conditions? Unquestionably, the facts were presented to them—perhaps not in official briefings but certainly by the men with whom they discussed conditions and operational problems. In fact, many of these men went out of their way to make sure that visiting officers from higher headquarters would learn what was going on, in the hope that corrective measures might be instituted. After leaving the Melbourne area, the three officers from Washington were to spend a period of five days at Townsville and on New Guinea with the foremost fighting unit in the southwest Pacific, the 22d Bomb Group, and there the "unblemished facts" were stated to them.‡

‡ Among those who talked to the visitors was Lieutenant Gerald J. Crosson, veteran pilot of many missions against the Japanese, and a man "who spoke his piece without any concern for the consequences."

One of the less dramatic but highly important phases of the special survey in Australia took place just outside Melbourne. The problems of supply were so acute that Anderson and Stevens were determined to investigate every possible way of easing the strain on the lengthy supply lines from the United States. They realized that any assistance in procuring supplies from local industry could have far-reaching effects on the conduct of the war. Since Johnson by this time was a close-knit member of the group, he went along with the two colonels to survey light industrial facilities outside Melbourne. These were being modified as rapidly as possible by the Australian government in order to permit the production of certain types of equipment for use by the American forces pouring into Australia.

After visiting a group of small plants, steel mills, and other factories, the three men found that each had come to almost precisely the same conclusions. As shown in Sam Anderson's notes, ". . . . it will be possible for this industrial capacity, limited as it is, to provide assistance to the supply problem through the local manufacture of small arms, ammunition, auxiliary equipment, and items such as sheet metal work in the repair of aircraft. Melbourne itself is too far south to be sought as a repair facility for combat aircraft; any such facility must be brought much closer to the fighting front."

By June 3, Johnson, Anderson, and Stevens agreed among themselves that it would be a waste of time to wait any longer for "The Swoose" to be declared fit to fly. The three officers arranged with Brett's headquarters to be flown north to Sydney on a commercial airliner of ancient Australian vintage.

Without military aircraft on hand to make travel possible on a convenient and definitely planned schedule, "we were tied down to the few and sorry commercial aircraft available at the time," Anderson said. Their desire now was to move northward and get into a combat area, with a combat organization, just as quickly as possible. But their rate of travel was not at all to their liking.

After spending the night of June 3 in Sydney's Australia House, early on the morning of the fourth§ they caught another commercial airliner to Brisbane, where the United States Navy's main base in Australia was located.

"There certainly wasn't much for the Navy to show in what was then the principal U. S. naval installation in Australia," Anderson recalled. "Johnson was delighted to act this time as our host because he was together with us for the first time on

§ June 4, 1942, was the start of the historic Battle of Midway, in which the United States Navy mauled the Japanese and broke the back of her carrier force. To Anderson, it was confirmation of the reason why his B-17E had been "commandeered" after the landing at Nouméa, New Caledonia.

a naval facility, but he quickly ran out of things for us to see. There were just a few vessels in the harbor—oh, perhaps a total of five submarines and tenders.

"We would have liked to have spent more time at Brisbane. We wanted to talk to the crews of the submarines, for we knew they were among the real unsung heroes of our war against the Japanese, and they were already well on their way in the astounding job they did on the enemy's shipping. What the Navy lacked in size and in strength down in the SWPA, they were trying to make up for with a grim, determined willingness to hit the enemy with everything they could throw together.

"Fortunately, we did manage to get some really excellent briefings from the Navy. The Battle of Midway had been shaping up for some time and, as we learned in the briefing, might explode into a wild and critical fight at any moment. If anything, that briefing brought home to us even more than we had realized the great distance involved in the Pacific, and the enormous magnitude of supplying our forces at the end of the lines from the United States."

But what created more of an impression upon the three observers was the repeated insistence on the need for better communications within the Southwest Pacific theater of operations. The officers of MacArthur's staff had placed the greatest stress on the need for improved communications in order to permit closer coordination not only among the different services but even among the major command echelons. And everything stated in the MacArthur staff briefings had been given even greater emphasis by the airmen of Brett's command.

This was natural enough, since it was the aircraft of the theater that moved the fastest, covered the greatest distances, contained the greatest potential for destroying the enemy, and, above all, would be subjected to possibly rapid changes in battle situations. This being the case, there was an urgent need to provide for an excellent exchange of data between air force units and other services. Unfortunately, even within the chain of command of the forces directly under Brett's control, there were great gaps and holes. Before all elements of the American forces and their Allies could be brought into even a semblance of well-coordinated activity against the Japanese, the lesser command echelons first had to be put into working order.

No matter how the situation was reviewed, the three visitors found it more than depressing: it contained the seeds of possible disaster. This was immediately evident to Anderson, who of the three had the greatest experience with long-distance, rapidly moving forces and who therefore knew only too well the consequences of having aggressive friendly forces in the same area—if none of those forces realized that an enemy might not be involved.

"Liaison between the air force units in Australia, and the Navy at Brisbane," Anderson related, "seemed to be either haphazard or even nonexistent. This was due directly to the lack of proper communications facilities, and the great distances between Brisbane and the widely dispersed air force installations. Yet, in view of what had happened in the immediate past, especially in the Coral Sea, we found this rather astonishing . . ."

The Battle of the Coral Sea, culminating on May 8, had made it painfully apparent not only that the United States lacked effective coordination between its land-based air power and its naval forces at sea, but that this very lack had proved to be damaging and possibly even fatal. The public did not, of course, know anything of this problem, since any revelations about this crack in our combat wall would have been of immeasurable comfort to the Japanese. Indeed, had the enemy known of some of the events that had occurred during the Battle of the Coral Sea, they might have celebrated even more exuberantly the results of that fight.

In a personal report dispatched under the highest security restrictions to Army Air Forces headquarters in Washington, Major General Ralph Roycell noted that

"We do not know where Naval vessels are . . . what they contemplate doing, nor when; all we know is that sometimes, with only a few hours' notice, we are asked to cooperate in some Naval operations . . . our striking force is now located along the railroad line from Townsville to Cloncurry. This necessitates flying the aircraft to Moresby for topping off before they can depart on the raid and flying that same distance back after the raid. This distance varies from six hundred to eight hundred miles. It means that we are using from three to five hours' fuel each way before the airplane ever starts on a mission. This also means that the airplanes must be flown to Moresby so as to arrive at dusk the day before the start of any scheduled mission. It is frequently impossible, therefore, to comply with Navy requests as they do not give us enough time to get to the topping off on the previous evening."[31]

This was substantially the problem, but it only hinted at the dangers inherent in the failure to coordinate activities between air force and naval units. Those dangers came to be realized in all their most ominous possibilities during the Battle of the

---

‖ One of Brett's top officers, Royce was a hardened combat veteran and known as a blunt, tough fighting man. He filed this report on the same day that Johnson, Anderson, and Stevens arrived in Melbourne; later he was to personally provide Johnson with a "startlingly blunt and revealing" briefing.

Coral Sea, when exhaustive studies of events during that struggle proved beyond any question that

". . . it is a matter of record, and we have the photographs, that we bombed our own Navy in the Coral Sea, simply because we did not have the information necessary to give our combat crews the positions of our own ships. There were no identification signals set up. It was our policy to bomb first and identify later. We knew the Japs were in there —but not our Navy. After that, however, we began to get intelligence from our Navy." [32]

On June 6, the news delivered to Johnson, Anderson, and Stevens was better—much better. The Battle of Midway had ended in disastrous defeat for the Japanese, who had lost four fast carriers, hundreds of planes, and their skilled crews.

But Midway was a great distance from Australia and New Guinea. More to the point, the Japanese were still adding to the numbers of planes they had already poured into the SWPA. On the fighting front—the sky the arena of battle—it was still a savage war in which the Japanese were taking a terrible toll of our outnumbered forces.

By noon on June 6, the three men were flying north from Brisbane in another commercial airliner. It was a bumpy, rocking flight punctuated with a series of landings at near-isolated small dirt airstrips. Their destination was Townsville, in northern Queensland. Just outside Townsville was Garbutt Field, headquarters for the 22d Bomb Group.

It was aboard a Marauder bomber of this Group that one of the three men was to meet a violent death.

CHAPTER FIVE

THE RAGGED WARRIORS

On the morning of June 7, Johnson, Anderson, and Stevens took off from Garbutt Field for a field tour of the different bases of the 22d Group. At long last they were free of the transportation problem: Anderson had his own hands on the control of a Lockheed C-40,* and his flight schedules depended entirely on his own actions. Johnson and Stevens were visibly relieved to be free of the constant waiting for airplanes, especially since they wished to visit three additional

* This plane was a military version of the twin-engined Lockheed that the Australians had been flying as a commercial airliner.

bases during the day, all but one of them (19th Bomb Group) manned by the 22d Bomb Group.

Sam Anderson was really in his element now. Being able to fly a plane was only part of it. Johnson and Stevens were delighted to see that the 22d Bomb Group and some of its personnel were old friends of Anderson; the colonel explained that before the war he had flown on a number of occasions with the 22d when they were first equipped with the Martin B-26 Marauder, a twin-engined medium bomber. It had been an exciting time—most pilots had been horrified when they first saw the B-26. Sleek, clean along every inch of her body, and with the biggest propellers and shortest wings of any military plane in the world, she was the hottest bomber in the air—and demanded the best in pilot skill.

Anderson was greeted warmly by Lieutenant Colonel Dwight Divine II, the new Group commander, and Lieutenant Walter A. Krell, one of the Group's outstanding pilots. Anderson and Krell had flown many hours together, and this was their first greeting since 1941. They met Lieutenant Gerald J. Crosson, one of the old-time pilots of the Group, who had ferried planes right from the production line of the Martin Company into Group service. Krell, Crosson, Divine, and a few of the old-line pilots of the 22d knew more about the Marauder than any other pilots in the country. This was a point of extreme interest not only to Anderson but to Johnson and Stevens. For the B-26 Marauder had begun to earn a reputation among a great many pilots as a killer. It was a hot airplane to fly; it landed with a speed almost as great as the cruising speed of other bombers. Men who flew the B-26 and were not sharp and did not stay right on top of the airplane could quickly get into trouble.

One outfit had so many crack-ups and accidents that the Air Force ordered every Marauder in the United States grounded at once until remedies for the accidents could be found.[33] President Roosevelt even before the outbreak of war had gone on record with his predictions of American bomber production; being forced to ground one of our prime weapons shortly after the war began did not speak well for his statements to the nation, for the company that produced the airplane, or for the Air Force officers who had ordered it into a "top priority mass production."

"There were a lot of pilots who called the Marauder a bitch and a killer," Anderson remarked, "but you could never prove it with guys like Walt Krell or Jerry Crosson. They were wild about the B-26; they loved that airplane. They could just about make the 26 sit up and sing songs to them. There were pilots in the States who dreaded flying in the B-26 under normal conditions. Krell, Crosson, and the other pilots in the 22d Bomb Group could fly that thing better on one engine—

which Stateside pilots often said was impossible—than most fliers could with both fans going."

The 22d Bomb Group and its men and facilities provided the three observers with an opportunity to obtain the best possible picture of the war against the Japanese, not simply in terms of combat reports or gripes about poor supply, but specifically and intimately by being with the men, by watching them work, by talking with them and actually participating in their activities.

Lyndon Johnson especially made a penetrating survey; Anderson has remarked that Johnson was a man who was absolutely determined to see things with his own eyes. The mechanics, gunners, pilots, and other men of the 22d Bomb Group with whom Johnson discussed their problems remember clearly—and confirm in individual recollections—that "this man asked us about our problems and our gripes; he wanted to know what we needed, what we were missing. He told us that he was here to find out what we needed so that he could help do something about it. He knew what he was talking about; his questions weren't hazy or general at all." [34]

Of course, the very sights about the air base spoke eloquently for themselves. As Sam Anderson noted carefully soon afterward, "We saw dispersed aircraft in what was virtually desert country . . . poor undergrowth, many scrub trees. People were living under very poor conditions, living in tents, and even those were often pretty frayed and in bad shape. They were critically short of maintenance equipment . . . particularly, sheet metal equipment for repairs. Even getting their planes repaired was a major task."

Johnson, Anderson, and Stevens walked along the desert paths. About them there were bombers standing without purpose, winged creatures chained to the ground awaiting long-overdue repairs. Their wings and bodies showed scars and gaping holes, and the visitors studied the black punctures where Japanese bullets and cannon shells had ripped through metal and through structural members, leaving the planes dangerously weakened until the metal could be made whole again.

The men who flew the Marauders were being mauled by the Japanese. There was a good reason for that, as Johnson was to learn from them first hand. For the B-26s, with their assignment of "wresting air superiority from the Japanese," found themselves the only planes flying consistently against the worst targets. And to do so, the men and planes were being stretched to their endurance limits, and then asked to perform beyond those limits. They were carrying out the missions of the four-engined B-17 heavy bombers (which were flying at thirty thousand feet and higher early in 1942 in order to survive), and the toll of men and machines was appalling.

"The rate of out-of-commission aircraft was about fifty per cent," said Anderson. "Fifty per cent of all the Group's planes were just waiting to be repaired so they could be thrown back into the battle. The Group was so short of crews that the men without planes simply took up other bombers that had been repaired. The fact that an airplane was out of commission didn't mean that its crew wasn't in there fighting almost constantly.

"The supply situation was absolutely terrible. Scavenging and improvisation was the order of the day. Stevens and Johnson were as shocked as I was—perhaps even more than myself, because I already had an idea of what to expect. Later, at the 19th Bomb Group, which flew B-17s, we found conditions, if this was possible, even worse. Their morale was terrible; their planes were flying wrecks. As far as a supply situation went, well, it was almost nonexistent. They were planning a mission while we visited their base, and the attempt to scrape together a bombing force was pitiful. They could get only *two* airplanes off the ground. It was terrible . . . I have never seen aircraft crews work under more adverse conditions."

Johnson, Anderson, and Stevens all took special pains to talk with as many of the crews as possible. They spent many hours with the mechanics, discussing their problems—including even a lack of tools with which to work, and a shortage of materials with which to improvise—and they learned how these men lived and worked, day and night, until some of them were numbed with fatigue and seemed to move like automatons. This was true not just in the area around Townsville but elsewhere.

Headquarters of the 22d Bomb Group, as well as the 19th Squadron, maintained its facilities at Garbutt Field. The 33d Squadron moved out to Antill Plains, some twenty miles south of Townsville. The 2d and 408th squadrons in turn went to Reid River, another twenty miles beyond Antill Plains.

From Garbutt Field on April 5, 1942, the 22d Bomb Group had taken off for its first strike against the powerful enemy bastion at Rabaul, on distant New Britain Island. This mission was the first in which any B-26 (in any theater) saw combat. It was also the first strike of medium bombers against the heavily defended base at Rabaul.

The team of Washington observers learned that, as bad as things were in northeastern Australia, they were considerably worse up at Seven-Mile Drome † on New Guinea, seven miles outside the harbor town of Port Moresby.

† Sometimes referred to by the crews as "Seven-Mile" or "Seven-Mile Strip."

Seven-Mile was the advance combat base through which the Marauders staged for refueling on their way to attack enemy targets. It was a crude, rough forward outpost, which the Japanese used for target practice several times a week, by day and by night; and bad as it was for the men who flew, it was sheer murder for those who patched and fixed and worked to keep the Marauders going.

Around Seven-Mile the world was basically unpleasant. In the summer the grass burned into brown straw, and the heat was wild, and so were the insects and especially the mosquitoes and the weird combination of choking dust from the airstrip and the dank humidity from the surrounding jungle and the sea. But even if it had been all neat and pretty, it would still have represented only agonizing tiredness to the ground crews.

When the Marauders came to Seven-Mile—staying sometimes to hit the enemy in a series of swift, hazardous raids— the ground crews knew a world limited strictly to bone-weary sleeplessness from working day and night, the groggy state into which they fell while they worked, broken only by the shriek of Japanese bombs or the stutter of cannon from Zeros sweeping up and down, strafing at treetop height.

The men who came back from the missions recall one time in particular, when they taxied down one side of the runway and spotted two Buddha-like figures in the parched grass on the far side. There, two mechanics—Sergeants Charles Fuqua and William H. Spiker—were sitting perfectly upright. Their legs were crossed beneath their bodies, and they were sound asleep.

These two men, if luck was with them, might average three hours' sleep a night when the raids increased in tempo. They considered five hours at any time a delectable luxury. Their bodies were caked with dirt, their hair with grease, their hands and faces with grime; cuts and scrapes and bruises marked their bodies because they worked on precarious mounts and used makeshift tools and their weary hands slipped into sharp metal.

Few men have ever shown their feelings about the ground crews more than Gerald J. Crosson, then a pilot with the 22d Bomb Group, or Walter Gaylor, who was with the 22d from June, 1941, through almost all of World War II.‡

"I'll never forget the men who worked on my plane and those of the squadron whenever we got to Moresby," Crosson asserted. "You see and experience a lot of things in a shooting

‡ Gaylor joined the 22d as 2d lieutenant, June, 1941, at Langley Field, Virginia; on June 9, 1942, he was made 1st lieutenant, adjutant of 33d Squadron; later, as major, was commanding officer of Headquarters Detachment, 22d Bomb Group.

war, and ours consisted of a lot of pretty wild shooting. But it was those men on the ground who really got to me.

"In the early days especially we didn't have any facilities for the mechanics and ground crews at Seven-Mile. The sun was pure hell. It came down on those people with an intensity that is just about impossible to describe. New Guinea under the best of conditions is only one step short of something for which you can develop a violent dislike, and these weren't the best of conditions.

"I've seen these men so battered by the sun that they couldn't work on the planes during daylight. We were even lacking the proper clothes for them to wear. More than a few had broken out in huge, painful blisters on their necks, across their backs, and on other parts of their bodies.

"Back in the States, they'd put a man into a hospital for something like that. Out here, they just kept right on working. But even the best of them couldn't remain in the blistering sun in that condition. So they'd knock off work and try to sleep during the day, in order to work the night through without that sun tearing them up."

Walt Gaylor picked up the story. "What Jerry describes is bad enough," he added, "but it doesn't tell how insidious this became for them. When the sun hammered down, it was just too hot to sleep. They had to lie on their stomachs, face-down, because of their burned backs and necks. And the sweat just poured off them.

"By night, with the sun down, they'd start to work. It was almost as hot, but at least they weren't being burned. But then came the mosquitoes . . . those eternally damned mosquitoes. And those poor guys couldn't wear shirts because of their blistered and raw skin, and there just wasn't any salve or medicine for them, and so the whole night through they'd fair go out of their minds—but they worked and they put those planes in shape. Sometimes they broke off work at night. That's when the Japanese hit us with bombers, and most everyone would run for the ditches and trenches. But not all. Some of those guys were so tired—the mechanics working on the airplanes—they said to hell with it and they kept working. We had to *order* them under cover.

"If they wanted to pick the real heroes of the 22d, for my money, these are the people."

There existed an amazing similarity of conditions from one airstrip to another around the Townsville area, from Garbutt to Antill to Reid River—a similarity of general wretchedness. As Anderson expressed it:

"What struck home most of all—to Johnson and Stevens, as well as myself—was the incredible morale of the men of the 22d Bomb Group. And this was despite something that didn't reflect credit on the Army Air Forces, or on the whole general military organization. These boys felt as though they had been written off by the United States. They were convinced that hardly anybody knew anything about them. I hate to say this, but it was largely the truth as far as the public was concerned. And despite all this, their morale was simply marvelous.

"The more we saw of the wretched conditions, the more amazed we became at the evidence of this high morale. It didn't seem possible that men could endure their privations, their terrible losses against the Japanese, their feelings of being abandoned by the United States, and still throw everything they had into the war against an enemy who outnumbered them, and against whom they fought without even a pretense at escort protection. There were also the so-called 'little things' that can sap the morale of a fighting outfit, which they endured.

"For example, the shortage of supplies was so bad, the men even had to scrounge their clothing. They were a motley-looking group, with patched clothes and odd combinations of attire. Some of the men flew their missions with Australian shorts, cowboy boots, and sport shirts, simply because there wasn't anything else to wear and they were glad to get this.

"This was the outfit that got a hot emergency call to go to war. On the morning of December 8, 1941, they were ordered out with such a critical call they didn't even have time to pack. As an indication of their dedication to duty, when they were told to get going and *at once*, they took their orders literally. They didn't stop to talk it over or question what was happening. Some of these pilots just ran out to their planes and even took off in their bedroom slippers. They never had the chance to return home to get their gear; they stayed on the move, and they ended up by having to scrounge for the clothes to wear on their backs.

"Johnson and Stevens were deeply impressed by what we saw. It was difficult—but wonderful—to reconcile the sights we ran across, in terms of their clothing, with their fabulous fighting record and their wonderful morale. Instead of looking shaggy, with their Australian bush hats and boots, and their wide grins, they even had a jaunty air about them."

The men with whom the Washington observers talked did not hold back their thoughts or their feelings. Death was always too close for them to be concerned about the niceties of protocol at the far ends of the earth. When someone from some distant but very much higher headquarters—someone who might be in the position to do something to help—came along, the crews just spilled their feelings and made their attitude clear.

Lyndon Johnson asked hard, fast questions. In conversations with ground crewmen, gunners, and B-26 crewmen of the 22d Bomb Group, he asked them to detail their problems, to share with him their thoughts and their conclusions. And they did exactly this—they laid it right on the line to the man with the lieutenant commander's stripes, the man whom few, if any of them, knew was also a Congressman.

There were other details about this amazing combat organization that were brought to the attention of Johnson, Anderson, and Stevens—details unknown even to the highest echelons of the Air Force or any other level of the military back in Washington. They were unknown because there was no one to spend the time or the effort compiling official histories or special reports, and the combat reports filed on the blank forms of the Royal Australian Air Force simply "disappeared."

The two colonels and the Navy commander wanted to know more about the way the men acted in combat. Since the Marauders of the 22d Bomb Group were facing the toughest opposition created over any target by the Japanese, this was an important factor in judging the effectiveness of our airmen under the worst possible conditions.

Lieutenant Louis W. Ford emphasized the fact that, in spite of the appalling losses suffered in combat against the Japanese,§ the Group had no choice but to continue driving deeply into the skies controlled by the enemy.

"The Japanese at that time," explained Ford, "enjoyed a solid air superiority over New Guinea. It was the lack of other forces to cope with this superiority that prompted the 22d Group to be assigned an air superiority role. I hesitate to be specific [today], of course, but it's completely accurate to say that our average losses approximated somewhere between 15 and 25 per cent per mission.[35]

"Some of our men were incredible. It was during this period that Carl King of the 33d Squadron gained quite a reputation for carrying along his toothbrush and brushing his teeth under attack. Jay Zeamer had quite a reputation also. He was in the 19th Squadron. He used to wear an old-fashioned helmet, the tin-hat kind. He would go to sleep—literally—while under fighter attack. One of the pilots once had Jay for a copilot and as the Zeros were blasting in and shooting them up, this pilot had to keep punching Zeamer on the chest to keep him awake as the Zeros were pouring bullets and cannon shells into the airplane.[36] Jay Zeamer was later shifted over to the 43d Bomb Group and his total lack of nerves earned him the Congressional Medal of Honor during a rough mission in the Solomons."

§ Ford himself was shot down on April 11, 1942, during a raid against Rabaul, New Britain. Six weeks later he and his crew walked out of the jungle to tell an incredible saga of survival.

Lou Ford then recalled some of the hours of 1942 and related the importance to the men of the Bomb Group of visits from higher headquarters: "Observers from the States and from high command were relatively few and far between. The lonely manner in which the group operated had created the conviction among our crews that we were carrying the United States side of the war load in the Southwest Pacific. The arrival of visiting dignitaries—and we considered them that—particularly those who had the guts to fly with us over the Japanese targets, reassured everybody that someone was paying attention to what was going on."

CHAPTER SIX

DECISION

While in Townsville the three-officer team stayed at the Buchanan, a wooden frame hotel two stories high, with each level fronted by a long, open porch running the length of the structure.

Townsville was sufficiently far to the north to be regarded as "pretty well up in the tropics." The rooms in the hotel were partitioned off, with only the thinnest of wooden walls separating them. Conversations in any one room were heard with clarity in the rooms adjoining. Even whispers could be heard through the walls—as was a conversation one afternoon between Lyndon Johnson and Francis Stevens.

On the day that the three men arrived at Garbutt Field and began their flying tour of the bases of the 22d and 19th bomb groups—Sam Anderson learned that June 9 was slated for the first major coordinated air strike against the Japanese at Lae airdrome, along the northeastern coast of New Guinea. Anderson immediately went to Dwight Divine, Group commander, and told him that he wanted to go along on the strike. Later that day, Anderson passed on the word to Johnson and Stevens about the scheduled mission. He added that he did not know if room would be available aboard other aircraft on June 9, but that it would be wise for them to check this out as soon as possible on their own—that is, if they wished to make the raid.

During the late afternoon of June 8, the voices of Lyndon Johnson and Francis Stevens could be heard by several people through the thin walls of the room in which Johnson and Stevens were talking. There was no mistaking the voices; nor was there any doubt about the topic under discussion. The subject was the mission set up for the following morning. Both Johnson and Stevens had decided that they were going along, no matter what the risks.

Sam Anderson was then elsewhere, but he knew—from Major General Bill Marquat—that Marquat personally attempted to dissuade Johnson from going. General MacArthur had declared to his staff that Lieutenant Commander Johnson as a Congressman was to have full VIP status, and the possibility that the first Congressman ever to visit the SWPA might be killed on a mission was not at all appealing to MacArthur.

The terrible casualties inflicted upon the 22d Bomb Group (as much as 15 to 25 per cent losses per mission), the miserable operational conditions, and the slim chances of survival on such a strike were all factors, Marquat insisted, that Johnson should consider most carefully. The general did not know what effect his cautionary remarks were having upon Johnson, but he was determined to talk the naval officer out of making the raid. However, Johnson (whom Marquat saw only as a Congressman) said flatly that he had come to the Southwest Pacific to "see personally for the President just what conditions were like, and I cannot find out what they *are* like if I don't go along on this mission." [37]

That conversation on June 8 was to prove ironic. As far as Johnson was concerned, there was nothing further to discuss. He was going—and that settled the matter. But, he insisted, there certainly was no reason for Stevens to risk his life, and he strongly advised his friend to remain at Port Moresby instead of flying on the mission. Stevens, he pointed out, was a ground-forces officer, and there was nothing that he could learn high above a Japanese field in New Guinea that would be important in any way to his particular mission on the survey trip.

Stevens brushed off the recommendation that he remain behind while Johnson and Anderson flew the raid. He told Johnson directly, "We agreed to stick together. If you two are going, then I am going too."

They dropped the subject there.

Less than eighteen hours later, Lieutenant Colonel Francis R. Stevens was dead.

CHAPTER SEVEN

DUCEMUS—"WE LEAD"

The 22d Bomb Group faced the toughest fighter opposition of any American air unit. The enemy fighter pilots based originally at Rabaul, and then also at Lae, were the killers of the famed Tainan Wing, the hand-picked, outstanding fighter pilots of the Japanese Navy. They included the top-scoring aces of Japan. That they were superb at the controls of their agile Zero fighters was not a matter of Japanese claims or of empty boasting. The men who would tell you of the Zeros that climbed out of Lae and ripped into American planes with grim effect were not Japanese. They were the survivors in the American bombers that came home, the fighter pilots who escaped the battles in which, most of the time, our pilots cursed their heavy planes as the Zeros whirled like dervishes about them.

That was the basis of the arguments advanced by General Marquat and other high-ranking officers in an effort to keep Lyndon Johnson out of one of the Marauders of the 22d Bomb Group. The chances were too high that he would be killed.

Every aspect of the mission from beginning to end was filled with danger—enemy fighters and flak, primitive maintenance, violent storms, mountainous conditions, and enough obstacles to make even a peacetime flight in the area something to give a pilot a sleepless night.

Lyndon Johnson had seen with his own eyes the problems of maintenance. He had spoken to the mechanics and the crew chiefs, the gunners and pilots, the operations officers, and the squadron leaders and group commander. These men had held nothing back in answering his questions or those of Anderson and Stevens. Perhaps the most eloquent example of "frenzied maintenance" was to be found in the scarred fuselage of one Marauder. The airplane seemed to be a flying wreck, but its crew stuck faithfully with the bomber—despite the fact that they had to jam a bedsheet into a gaping hole in the fuselage and fly that way for a week until sheet metal could be scrounged to make effective repairs.

The 22d Bomb Group, then, was the organization with which Johnson was to fly into battle, the men with whom he was to face enemy guns; on that occasion, unknown to him, the sudden decision of a Japanese pilot to attack a second formation of Marauders was to probably save the bomber in which Johnson was flying.

Thus, five days in the combat history of the men and the Marauders of the 22d Bomb Group—from June 6 to June 10—are also five of the most compelling days in the life of Lyndon Johnson.

In order to fly a mission against the Japanese, the men who flew the Marauders from northeastern Australia had to overcome a series of formidable obstacles. The twin-engined bombers first took off from their home fields of Garbutt, Reid River, and Antill, loaded with bombs and full ammunition belts, and began the long overwater flight to Seven-Mile Drome near Port Moresby, New Guinea. The planes landed at Seven-Mile to refuel and receive scanty and generally unreliable weather reports and briefings that had a 50-50 chance of being accurate.

This was the only way that we could carry the war to the enemy. It meant, however, that these bombers had to fly a total round-trip distance of twenty-six hundred miles simply to attack Lae. Thirteen hundred of those miles were flown with full bomb loads; twenty-four hundred of them were flown over open and shark-infested waters.

"There were so many sharks in the sea between Townsville and Moresby," explained Jerry Crosson, "that we could fly low and actually see their fins and bodies cutting the water. Sometimes we went down real low, right on the deck, and the gunners would cut loose with their fifties. The crews behind us told us later, after landing at Moresby, that they could see the water frothing and even turning red from the sharks attacking those that we'd killed and wounded with our machine guns."

One B-26 badly hit over Lae on May 26 managed to get as far as the coast, while the crew slipped into their parachutes with frantic haste. Four men made it into the water. The Japanese pilot Saburo Sakai, the leading ace of the Tainan Wing at Lae, circled the men, who were only two miles from his field. Then he became witness to an incredible sight:

"Suddenly one of the men thrust his hands high above his head and disappeared. The others were beating fiercely at the water, and trying to get into their raft. Sharks! It seemed that there were thirty or forty of them; the fins cut the water in erratic movements all about the raft. Then the second man disappeared. I circled lower and lower, and nearly gagged as I saw the flash of teeth which closed on the arm of the third man. The lone survivor, a big, bald-headed man, was clinging to the raft with one hand and swinging wildly with a knife in the other. Then he, too, was gone. . . ." [38]

Even flying over New Guinea was a tremendous adventure, for the mountain range jutted to well above ten thousand feet. The passes through which the planes sometimes tried to slide were rarely below seven thousand feet, and thick, turbulent clouds often covered the area.

At Moresby itself, the only strip that could handle the Marauders was Seven-Mile. "Everything there was primitive," related John Richardson, 22d Bomb Group operations officer. "All about the field were the mountains, matted over with a pestilent jungle growth. The hills and mountains were inhabited with treacherous natives, and there was always a ruthless enemy to contend with. Moresby proper was a malaria-infested hole at the time. The crews had to bring their own bedding and mosquito bars. Since no adequate living quarters of *any* kind were available, the men slept—or tried to sleep—the night through beneath the wings of their planes. Since the Japanese would hit us without warning at night, two men always slept in their plane—ready to kick over the engines and rush the bombers to dispersal points. The food consisted of emergency rations. There was no radar, and there were no sirens, and our air raid warning consisted of an alarmed sentry firing three shots rapidly into the air. If you didn't hear the shots, the next sound you usually heard were the bombs whistling down toward you.

"During daylight, the air raid warning signal was a bit different. Someone frantically hoisted a red flag atop the rickety operations tower (it was made of logs and was a laugh) and if you saw the tower guys themselves come tumbling down and scooting off in all directions, why—you might even have two or three minutes to run and throw yourself into a deep ditch or any hole around. We were pretty fond of some of the old bomb craters.

"There were no revetments for the dispersed planes, and to save them, pilots often took off with cold motors and with bombs raining down as they went along the runways. And then there were the Zeros, which could always be counted upon to come right down to the runway and strafe everything and anything."

Maps? "What are those?" the crews would mutter. There were maps every now and then, but they were a rarity rather than a normal part of operations. When the men finally did get them, they soon threw them away in disgust because the information was so inaccurate.

Weather forecasting was almost nonexistent, and more than once entire formations were turned back from their targets because of violent—unpredicted—storms.

Over the Owen Stanley Range particularly the weather was treacherous. Frequent storms, vicious downdrafts, and often impenetrable mists claimed more than a few planes and their entire crews.

The intensity of the Japanese attacks against Moresby was increasing (another worry of MacArthur's staff officers was that Johnson would be caught on the ground in a heavy enemy strike). During the month of May alone—just before Johnson arrived to spend his five days with the 22d—the Seven-Mile Drome received no less than twenty-one separate and major bombing attacks. These were carried out with forces that included in a single raid as many as thirty-four bombers with fifteen escorting Zeros. Many of the combat reports (written in haste because there was no one who could be spared to serve as Group historian) simply stated "considerable damage to Seven-Mile Drome" and described in brief statistics how many men were killed or wounded, and how many planes destroyed or damaged. It was common and the men expected it to happen at any time.

The crews remember one take-off at three o'clock in the morning from Seven-Mile Drome. No one liked to try to get off Seven-Mile at night—it was bad enough racking a B-26 into the air from that field during the day. No one knew, either, exactly how long the strip was. Some people claimed that it was five thousand feet from one end to the other; others said that it was only four and a half thousand feet. But they all agreed that it could have been longer and considerably better.

The strip at Seven-Mile was what the pilots called an "uphill-downhill thing and there were times when it could get pretty hairy." Above all, the pilots did not want any part of the uphill take-offs, because of the load to be carried and the condition of the runway. At one end of the runway there was a small hill, and if the temperature was high they needed a lot more speed and distance than usual to get safely into the air.

But sometimes they did not have the speed, and maybe the wind was blowing from the wrong direction—or maybe it shifted after the plane began its take-off roll. Along the runway were dull, small ground flares; not very many of them—barely enough to keep a man going in the right direction. Every flare had someone standing by to douse it immediately if the Japanese came over suddenly.

That crew's three-o'clock take-off made the other pilots wish they could forget they had ever seen it. The Marauder sailed into the darkness, her exhausts spitting dull flame. Just as she was over the grove of trees at the end of the runway, pulling for altitude, something happened—no one knows what, of course—and the darkness vanished before a mushrooming ball of orange flame.

Then a vicious blast ripped through the trees, giving the body of each man on the strip a squeeze as the pressure wave thrust its way past them. The sharp, roaring sound brought signs of relief to the faces of the watching men. The roar meant that the bombs in the plane had exploded and that any survivors in the wreckage had been mercifully released in that shattering instant. Death was a blessing, the men said; burning alive was every kind of known hell.

Walt Krell had some memorable comments to make on Seven-Mile Drome. Of greater significance, however, is the fact that Walt Krell's extensive notes, taken during this phase of the war, show more starkly and deeply the nature of conditions at the time:

"Seven-Mile used to get laced by the Japs two or three times every few days, and the bomb craters would get refilled with gravel, sand and earth, uncompacted. This would allow the heavily laden wheels of the B-26 to rut and sink. With about nine inches of propeller clearance from the ground even on a hard surface, you can well imagine the amount of pebbles we nicked the props with as we wallowed around trying to get lined up in this soft dry mush, with landing struts compressed under a full load of bombs, ammo, fuel and crew. A number of times we had to take off downwind and we'd clip grass for a mile or more getting the wheels up and bleeding up the flaps before we really could figure we were flying. Nothing like a good thrill first thing—why wait to get to the target?

"The B-17 and B-25 pilots didn't quite have this problem of the tremendously high wing-load factor of the B-26 and they couldn't seem to understand why we griped so much about the runway. After I explained that we were running short of pilots and having to borrow Aussies, and that arrangements undoubtedly could be made to have some of the B-17 and B-25 pilots transferred to the 22d Group and B-26s, we heard no more queries about why the B-26s didn't clear the runway as easily as the other types of aircraft."

When reports reached Australia from the United States that there had been so many accidents with the B-26 that it had been ordered grounded, MacArthur's staff (and that of Brett, of course) were fully aware that the bulk of their bomber force was made up of the same airplane. The crews' reaction to being forced to fly an airplane in battle that was deemed unsafe to get off the ground in the States was not something pleasant to contemplate.

They need not have worried. When the men of the 22d Bomb Group heard the news about the "killer B-26s ordered on the ground" back Stateside, they howled with laughter. "Send 'em to us!" one tailgunner chortled. "We'll take all we can get. They can keep the rest of their crumby airplanes." [39]

The record has never been set straight in this matter. Perhaps it might never have been brought to light again except that Lyndon Johnson flew on a combat mission against the Japanese in this type of aircraft.

The *only* reliable source of information concerning the effectiveness of the Marauder as a combat weapon must be the men who flew the plane in battle. Lieutenant Crosson, who flew B-26 Serial Number 01422 with the 2d Squadron of the Group, and who was also an outstanding engineering test pilot, has conclusive opinions about the Marauder:

"For a long time I've been fed up with the stories that the B-26 had peculiar characteristics, or was too hot to handle, or was too much for one pilot. There have been all sorts of stories told about the airplane. And most of them are just so much nonsense.

"My first experience with the Marauder was 'way back in June of 1941, at Wright-Patterson Field in Ohio. I personally have more than fifteen hundred hours in the B-26 and I've loved every minute of them. It was a fabulous machine.

"Sure, the plane met with mixed reactions at first. People who loved to fly a good airplane were wildly enthusiastic about it. It demanded a lot of its pilots, but it also gave them more in return than any other airplane flying.

"Now, the old men of the Air Corps didn't like the B-26. It made them work; it demanded that they be sharp. The Martin Company was so far ahead of its time that many pilots weren't ready, on a wide scale, for the airplane. Even by today's standards, the '26 is a beautiful piece of machinery.

"It was like a big pursuit plane . . . she was absolutely responsive to the controls. If you knew what you were doing, she never gave you any sudden or unexpected surprises. I've flown about every hot ship the Air Force ever had and the B-26 is right at the top of the list as one of the finest I've ever flown.

"A great many of the brass that came to visit us in Australia and up at Seven-Mile wanted to know just how we felt about the airplane. They'd heard it was a 'killer.' When we learned that the Air Force even grounded them for a while in the States, we could hardly believe the news. Because our airplanes were taking a terrible beating, and even the Japanese respected the machine, she was so fast.

"The B-26 was incredibly strong, and packed into a long, beautiful shape. I've seen holes as big as beer barrels in the wings and it didn't bother that bird a bit. It was a real military machine—a *weapon*.

"Early in June we had the brass at our field at Reid River; the three officers from Washington on a field survey trip were paying particular attention to the airplane and the 'problems' we were supposed to be having with it. We talked quite a bit with Anderson, of course. Johnson was unmistakable; tall, in Navy uniform. We'd had some Navy people with us for a while when we were training to fly the Marauder in torpedo attacks. But they'd been gone from our outfit for a while when Johnson came through with his group.

"They asked us questions about the Marauder, not in terms of her general characteristics, but when the going got rough. They had heard so much about the B-26 and the fact that she couldn't fly on only one engine that they must have had some pretty strong doubts in their minds. Well, whoever told them the '26 couldn't fly with only one fan going is clear out of his mind.

"I flew one home all the way back from Lae with one engine shot up and dead. Hell, I've made dozens of flights with one of those props feathered—and I'm talking about the original '26 with the short wings. Arkie Greer and John Richardson dragged over the mountains one day with only one engine going. And they weren't the only guys in our outfit to climb out with a full load, including bombs, with one engine dead. . . ."

John Richardson, operations officer of the 22d, recalled the occasion: "Everything seemed to fall apart on us that day. We lost an engine right after take-off. We were really loaded with fuel, bombs, and everything else. We were marginal all the way, of course, but on only one engine we dragged ourselves over the hills until we got out over the water—beyond Seven-Mile at Moresby—and we could salvo our bombs safely. So even if things got real bad for you, that Marauder was enough of a brute to drag you on out of trouble."

"But of all the things we liked best about the B-26," added Crosson, "the nicest was its speed. We would get up to three hundred miles per hour indicated, right on the deck, and that is true speed. It was just about as fast as most fighters flying at the time. Many times in combat we shoved over into long dives—a very steep gliding angle would be closer to it—and we would indicate three hundred and sixty miles per hour, and that was enough to give the Zeros a real hard time in trying to stay with us.

"Some of the guys, of course, when they were being shot to ribbons, would pound toward the ocean, trying to get to the water with everything in the cockpit shoved all the way forward, and in their dives they would indicate over four hundred miles per hour. The airplane is supposed to start coming apart at the seams when you do things like that, but ours never did, even when they were all shot up and with holes all over them. The Zeros couldn't turn to make their pursuit passes at us. The moment they turned when we were hell-bent for leather we'd pull ahead of them."

Richardson expanded on that point. "I was on one mission when it seemed that the Zeros picked us out as their particular target," he said. "They shot us to ribbons. They hit us at their leisure until we completed our bomb run. Not until then were we able to start running downhill, to run for home and build up our speed. I don't know how we ever got back.

"That B-26 was a flying wreck. It shook and buffeted from all the gaping holes and the jagged pieces of metal sticking out into the wind. We were really pouring the coal to the airplane and we were 'way over the maximum permissible speed, and we were still doing our very best to squeeze even more out of the machine. If we had been in any other airplane, we would never have made it."

Captain John N. Ewbank, Jr.,* one of the "old veterans" of the 22d Bomb Group, was another pilot who knew, and trusted, the Marauder as few other men ever did.

"The difference between the B-26 and the B-25†—and it was the kind of comparison you simply couldn't avoid, I suppose," he said, "equates sort of the difference between a Cadillac and a Ford. The B-26 was put together beautifully. I really mean that. Its skin was matched with wonderful precision, without metal overlapping on the outside, with everything wonderfully flush and smooth. The pilot's cockpit was a pilot's dream. The seat moved wonderfully to whatever position you wanted, and for long missions that meant a great deal to the man in that seat. The automatic pilot was far superior to the one in the B-25.

"Now don't misunderstand me on any of this—I'm *not* knocking the B-25. That was a great weapon, as was the B-26, but the B-25—the Mitchell—was extremely austere. It was a jitney, you might say, but nevertheless a very capable airplane and outstanding as a weapon. It was just that everything in the B-26 spelled quality and superb workmanship in capital letters.

"All this lends itself to combat characteristics, for we would fly the pants off a B-25. We had that short-winged B-26 and except for a few fighters we could outrun anything in the air. We could carry a bomb load about as big as that for a B-17 and a lot faster, although not as high or as far, of course.

"But in terms of the medium bombers, every one of us preferred the B-26 to anything else ever built. It was unbelievably rugged. We brought them home smashed and battered,

* He is now a brigadier general and the Deputy Assistant Director of Operations, Tactical Air Command, USAF.

† This twin-engined, twin-tailed medium bomber was widely used in World War II, and had an exceptional combat record throughout the world.

we bellied them in when our gear systems were shot away, and three days later or sooner they were back in combat, slugging it out and taking everything dished out to us.

"For my money, it was the finest weapon we had. It's too bad we didn't have more of them. And, as well, the spare parts and mechanics and the crews to really give us a chance to concentrate more on the enemy than spending so much time scrounging parts and jury-rigging repairs so that we could get back into the air and fly our missions. . . ."

The observers from Washington listened, and learned, and dismissed once and for all the rumors about the Marauder that had drifted through different channels back in the States. There could be no argument with the men who faced the enemy under brutal conditions and who came home to insist that the Marauder was the "finest weapon" we had. Did they have any gripes about their situation? They had plenty of these, about supplies and runways and critical shortages, but, as Jerry Crosson said, "nothing that more crews, mechanics, supplies, and more B-26's couldn't fix."

CHAPTER EIGHT

THE ANGRY SKIES

"Who was the nut who told everybody back in the States that the Japanese were no match for us in the air? Those Japanese we met over New Guinea and up at Rabaul weren't just *good*—they were hell on wheels. They were real good. We never had a doubt in the world that we were slugging it out with the cream of the crop. And Lae was about the worst of all. You were raked over the hot coals just about every single time you made *that* haul over the mountains. Remember those missions, John?"

John Richardson waved a hand at John Ewbank. Ewbank leaned back; he did not have to try hard to remember the missions over New Guinea and New Britain. He had said more than once that you *never* forgot what it was like in the skies of the southwest Pacific . . .

"Yeah, Rabaul was really something. There was only one way to think of that target. Rabaul would really shake you up whenever you went up there to try your luck."

Ewbank let his thoughts drift, then sat up suddenly. "It was rugged, real rugged. Those Japanese were some damned fine flying people, let me tell you.

"There was a run against Lae when I was convinced we would never make it back home. The mission called for us to make the flight to the target right on top of a cloud deck, and then to break through and go busting over Lae. Hit them with complete surprise.

"I led that mission. Everything was going fine; we thought we really had it made. But all of a sudden we had company. Those pilots at Lae were always hungry for bear, it seemed. Call them—well—'exceptionally aggressive' is as good a term as any, I suppose. Far as I was concerned, they were out to tear us to pieces.

"This was the first mission I was ever making when the Zeros ringed me in. I thought we had full surprise, and the funny thing is, we *did*. But the moment we were in sight we could see activity ahead of us. We were really moving too. By the time we got to the end of the runway I was staring at those Zeros scrambling into the air like a swarm of gnats. They just hauled those planes right up at us, and they came gunning for us straight out of their take-off runs. I'd never seen anything like it.

"We went low over that field, bombs cascading down from us, and our gunners not knowing whether to shoot up the targets on the field or to try and track those Zeros that were clawing at us. Soon as we got the bombs out, I turned sharply and led the formation down low over the water. But the Zero pilots acted like they were pretty mad because they hadn't been able to stop the attack. When we turned to head for home they cut inside real tight and fast and then they were all over us.

"They stayed with us and gave us hell. That was also the first time I brought my airplane home a flying wreck, we were so full of gashes and holes. They really gave us a going-over. They came in to point-blank range like our gunners weren't even there, and then they hosed everything they had at us. And they had plenty . . ."

In the weeks preceding the mission that Johnson, Anderson, and Stevens planned to fly, the 22d Bomb Group had been taking a particularly rough mauling from the Japanese at Lae. But so had the other outfit flying medium bombers; the 3d Bomb Group flew B-25 Mitchells against the crack fighter pilots who rose from Lae to do battle—and they, like the Marauders from the 22d, were being slashed and bloodied in devastating fashion.

On May 23 a single B-25 was pounded into flaming wreckage, disintegrating in the air and falling in small pieces toward the ocean. The Zero pilot from Lae, unknown to the Americans, of course, was Japan's then-leading ace, Saburo Sakai.[40] His extraordinary skill as a pilot and his accuracy with his guns and cannon had spread his fame across the

Pacific and throughout Japan, where (without his knowledge at the time) he had become a national hero. His superb combat flying chalked up a grisly toll of fighters and bombers. What boded ill for the unsuspecting American bomber crews was the fact that the fighter wing at Lae contained several other highest-scoring aces, along with Sakai.

On May 24 the American bombers suffered a particularly severe setback. Eight B-25s of the 13th Squadron, 3d Bomb Group, were led by their commander, Captain Herman F. Lowery, against Lae. There was no fighter escort. Lowery took his bombers through a pass in the Owen Stanley Range, swept wide of the Salamaua air base substation, and then swung in from the east to attack Lae. But when he started his run against the target, he discovered that two of his bombers had dropped out of the formation. The six B-25s steadied down for their bomb run.

Eleven Zero fighters met them head-on. They included some of the best pilots at Lae, and they slaughtered the American planes.

Lowery's B-25 was jumped almost at once by a Zero piloted by Hiroyoshi Nishizawa.* Under a short burst of cannon shells the B-25 exploded and smashed into the ocean as a ball of fire. Toshio Ota shot down the second Mitchell. Moments later, Saburo Sakai tore the third American bomber into disintegrating wreckage. Junichi Sasai's guns blew up the fourth B-25. Saburo Sakai came into point-blank range to rip the fifth plane into burning wreckage, his second kill of the fight.

The pilots then crowded against the last B-25, cutting it to ribbons before they finally broke off their attack and went back to Lae. Somehow, with their airplane almost falling apart about them, the crew managed to get back to Moresby, where the pilot crashed his airplane on the strip.

Five out of six . . . Small wonder that General Marquat was doing his level best to keep Lyndon Johnson out of any airplane that had Lae as its target.

There's a strange postscript to the disastrous mission of May 24. It is told in these pages for the first time, by a man who was then a lieutenant with the 22d Bomb Group. Walter A. Krell himself was considered one of the greatest bomber pilots ever to take to the air. He was a man who drove himself mercilessly. War correspondent Pat Robinson said of him: "If ever a man subordinated himself to his crew, it was Krell. To

---

* Nishizawa became the ace of aces of Japan, with a total number of kills of 102 enemy planes, according to former Commander Tadachi Nakajima, who was also at Lae. Ironically, Nishizawa was shot down while flying an unarmed transport, ferrying a group of pilots in the Philippines to an airfield to pick up new fighter planes.

him, leadership was more than a responsibility; it was a consecration to those who served with him." [41]

Walt Krell made a meticulous examination of the combat records of the Lae fighter wing; especially the reports by Saburo Sakai. And then he recalled the past: "much too vividly," as he said.

He had compared his own flight log with those of the Japanese pilot. "As I go back through all this," he said, "a thousand and one incidents flash through my mind. As I thumb through Sakai's records covering this period of the war, almost every page comes to life with episodes with which we were so terribly familiar. For example, Sakai details the great day they had when they knocked down five out of six B-25s.

"I was worried that the Japs had come up with some sort of a new gimmick that gave them some kind of tremendous odds. I was particularly concerned because I was scheduled to take the next Group flight over Lae where this had happened. After some effort, I got next to some 3d Group pilots, but they couldn't seem to do a thing but lament what they thought was in store for them on their next trip over the target.

"Weeks later, a very thin, little, blond pilot wearing dark glasses came to Woodstock, seeking a ride south. He was going blind, and was on his way to a General Hospital in Melbourne. Combat was over for him.

"He was Don Mitchel, an old friend and classmate of mine, *the sole survivor of the five bombers shot down on May 24.* He told a fantastic tale, too long to go into now, except that he was riding in the copilot's seat, the formation got split, his ship was being shot up—both engines out and burning, the cockpit full of smoke, everybody yelling, nothing working—when somebody hollers, 'Bail out!'

"Don remembered that somebody jerked the emergency release panel over his head. He stood up on his seat, getting ready to leave, when somebody gave him a powerful boost on the fanny, and shoved him clear of the ship. He jerked madly on the D-ring of his parachute; the silk banged open with a terrific jerk. Don must have been right on the deck when he went out. He was still in mid-air when his ship hit the water with a roaring explosion. His body then made only one swing and he was in the water himself. He looked toward his plane, but all he could see was that little cloud of steam the planes would leave when they went down.

"Now for the payoff. His legs were useless, having been injured somehow. He was several miles offshore, and a few of the Zeros came down after him. They strafed him repeatedly while he kept pushing himself underwater to duck. Finally they got tired of the game or figured he was dead, and flew away.

"Don was in the water for a long time before some natives picked him up. How he got back over the Owen Stanley Range to Port Moresby without the use of his legs is a fantastic story all in itself."

Krell paused for a moment. "You know, it's particularly interesting for me to get Sakai's point of view, since it's nice to know that we weren't the only people in the air to be worried over New Guinea. Sakai tells of a Zero pilot who was determined to get a B-26 by ramming; he even gives his name —Suitsu.

"Don't question what Sakai says about this because, believe me, *I know*.

"I remember this guy coming in from the right front. There was a flight of four B-26s on me, and another flight of four right behind. I kept waiting and waiting for this guy to fire so I could kick the formation down and spoil his aim. I'll be hanged if this Zero didn't slide right over the left wing of my airplane. He was nearly inverted, and still trying to pull down. Had he been a little more on center, he might have clipped our tail, but he missed us and slammed into Moe Johnson's ship.

"Joe Morningstar and I went over the full report by Saburo Sakai. He tells how the Zero, after the collision, went through a series of slow rolls and went into the sea at full speed. Then he describes how the B-26, without its vertical fin, yawed and rolled crazily, flipped over on its back, and plunged into the water with what Sakai called a blinding explosion.

"Well, he's right. Every single detail checks out; there isn't a shred of conflict about that episode as the Japanese pilot told it—and as we saw it.

"Not until I saw Sakai's story did I know why I wasn't killed myself on that mission."

Several days after the loss of the five B-25 Mitchell bombers, Lieutenant Colonel Divine, commander of the 22d Bomb Group, wrote in his diary:

"The lads had some tough luck today. Five went over Lae —two from 18th Sq. were Ellis and O'Donnell, two from 33rd were Coleman and Lanford, and there was Burnside from the 19th. Ellis' ship was riddled, the navigator (Kallina) killed. O'Donnell lost an engine, came all around the tip of New Guinea to get back and landed two hours late. Coleman's ship made emergency landing at Moresby. Lanford crashed into the ocean on fire near Lae. Bad show, and for several reasons. Moresby must not have given them any definite plan, and no one was in charge. Bad."

There was this entry for the day following:

"May 28th, 1942. ———— came back today, and gave me

some dope on his mission. He said he doesn't want to go over Lae again without fighter cover, and I certainly don't blame him. . . ."

The bombers had it rough, but our fighter pilots were little better off in their struggle with the Japanese Zero. Nothing tells of this situation more eloquently than this excerpt from the official records of a fighter squadron:

"The 67th didn't attack; it was attacked . . . The Zeros dived down around a cloud and then zoomed up into the six P-400's † from behind and below . . . The P-400's started turning into a Lufberry, but there were more Zeros than there were P-400's. Then the Grumman Wildcats came down from above and hit the Zeros. The mix-up began. Zeros were everywhere, zipping, darting and twisting, climbing straight up, and practically making square turns. The 67th pilots, in their heavy, lumbering P-400's, *felt like a herd of cows being attacked on every flank by agile wolves.*

"It was impossible to shake the Zeros by trying to maneuver. The only way was to head down into a cloud, make a turn on instruments, and come out on top. Then try to get a burst at a Zero before three others jumped you. All over the sky P-400's were running for the clouds . . ." [42]

Walt Krell more than any other one man, state the members of the 22d Bomb Group, had a deep and intimate sense of identification with the job that he, the other pilots, and the crewmen were expected to carry out in the war against the Japanese. The sense of identification, an unflinching devotion to the uniform he wore, enabled Krell to record, through the years, the words that best describe what the angry skies over New Guinea were like:

"There were many struggles in that war," Krell said. "And it's still amazing to me, after all the years have gone by, how many of them had to be fought just to get the airplanes off the ground and on their way to the target. At the end of a long line of obstacles, of which more than a few were maddening to people who were overworked and overtired, and who saw no way out of the maw of continuous missions . . . well, at the end of it all waited the Japanese. There were moments when they seemed to be only part of that great over-all picture so glibly described as the 'enemy.'

"For the lads hanging around under the wings of the B-26s, waiting for the word to go, a lot went on in the Operations Shack they never knew about. For example, time and again I would be ordered to depart Townsville with a flight of six, eight, or ten ships, having been told by the Group Powers that

† The P-400 was an export model of the Bell P-39 Airacobra fighter; the P-400 had a 20-mm instead of a 37-mm nose cannon, and was slightly inferior in performance to the P-39. Many AAF outfits, however, were equipped with the export model.

no specific targets were known. All we were told was to hit some enemy point like Lae or Rabaul. Nothing else; what kind of a way was that to fight a war!

"Once in Port Moresby, I would again check with Aussie Intelligence, only to find that their reconnaissance planes had picked up nothing new in the way of targets. Time and time again our missions resolved themselves into nothing more than raids to expose ourselves to ground fire and the engagement of Zeros, with no specific ground targets. And no matter what size bombs we used, we were never able, it seemed, to tear up their runways enough to prevent the Zeros from getting off the ground.

"In the absence of specific targets and because the Japanese on the 90-mm antiaircraft guns were awfully good, I sometimes decided to take the flights through the target area flying defensively instead of holding a straight and level course. Our aircraft losses were far exceeding our replacements as it was and, from the standpoint of pursuing the war, I couldn't reconcile the deliberate and prolonged exposure of a standard bombing run on nothing but a strip of dirt with 100-pound bombs.

"We had been told that most of the enemy installations and stores were concealed some distance back from the runways—just where, no aerial photo ever seemed to show. I reasoned that anywhere that our bombs may hit within working distance of the runway may do good and, at the same time, obviate the straight and level flying.

"One time at Lae we set off an ammo dump that nobody seemed to know was there—except the Japs. Often the boys on my wings couldn't see this philosophy, and I was criticized for not following the standard textbook Emily Post procedure for delivering bombs. The facts were that, when we did have something to go after, we did follow the instruction book on the Norden bombsight.

"Because of this lead policy of mine, there were certain crews and craft on hand to fly another day, when our purpose was of greater import than 'Douglas MacArthur's Smashing Raids' headlines. The low-level attacks really came into their own a little later, when ordnance came out with the delayed fuse. Often our sheet-metal people had more work to do patching up holes from our own bomb shrapnel than from enemy ground fire.

"All the foregoing is background for the idea that as combat airmen we didn't think we were doing any good because of the obscure and elusive targets. We felt like misfits and stepchildren. In fact, it wasn't until George Kenney came over to command the new Fifth Air Force later in 1942—that guy was a real cock-of-the-walk—that we started to get some true indication that people really knew we were even in the Southwest Pacific and fighting pretty much of a wild war down there.

"Any semblance of organization or leadership from the Group level on up to Air Force level was pure fiction. At one time our own Group even received orders, in the middle of all that miserable way of life and the staggering losses we were taking, that commissioned officers would carry swagger sticks and grow mustaches and that squadron commanders would not fly combat. We'd heard all kinds of weird things, but this really topped it off. I leave to your imagination just how much attention we paid to *that*.

"General Brett was barely on speaking terms with MacArthur. There was a host of old Air Corps brass dumped into our combat area who negated, confused, and compounded problems by the score. It took several months of operation to weed this latter group out, away from the forward combat areas.

"In the final analysis, it was the persistence of the individual pilot and his crew to get to the target that kept the war alive and the enemy engaged. We were, very simply, doing our best. It wasn't a matter of being gung-ho; it was a lousy war and things were rough no matter how you looked at it.

"Time gives you perspective. But one truth hasn't changed a bit. The determination and resourcefulness of the flight crews and the ground crews was the greatest single deciding factor in relation to the number of times a plane got out on a mission."

There's a certain medal that few men in uniform wear. It is known as the Soldier's Medal, and it is one of the most universally respected awards any man may hold. It is the medal awarded to those men ". . . who distinguish themselves by heroism not involving actual conflict with the enemy . . . for the performance of an act of heroism involving voluntary risk of life under conditions other than those of conflict with the enemy."

One day at Seven-Mile Drome a B-26 came back to the strip, almost staggering through the air. It was badly shot up—more a flying wreck than a sleek bomber. It lurched dangerously as it came down from the sky toward the runway. And then it did stagger, and smashed against the unyielding earth, sliding down the runway with a terrifying screech of flame-engulfed metal.

Almost all the crew got out. But the copilot was trapped, and the flames tore at his flesh. His pilot stood in the fire, struggling madly to get his friend out of the airplane. It was too late; the copilot died, but not before the pilot himself suffered third-degree burns from the hips down.

They gave the pilot the Soldier's Medal.

He was the same man who led the mission on June 9, the one on which Lyndon Johnson flew.

It was quite a man who led that raid. No question about it; his name was Walter A. Krell.

CHAPTER NINE

FINAL PREPARATIONS

From June 6 through June 8, the three-man team of observers studied the 22d Bomb Group as it prepared for the first co-ordinated air attack of the war in the Southwest Pacific against the Japanese.

The historian of the Group (an adjutant doubling in brass every now and then to keep some kind of headquarters report) noted with a touch of irony: "This awe-inspiring operation is to include the entire Army Air Corps striking force available in the Southwest Pacific. One can imagine how we all look forward to this blow that 'might end the war.' " [43]

Nothing tells the story better than the official log of Headquarters, 22d Bomb Group, for the days of June 7 and 8:

"June 7th: Activities today centered on planning the operation for Tuesday. We are kingpin, according to Garing [Australian], and the main purpose of the whole operation is to get our B-26's hard on target. Therefore, it's our task to make the plans that will include the scheduling and operation of the other aircraft as well. The B-17's and the B-25's will comply with our requirements. The plan is to have the three B-17's go from Horn [Island] direct to Lae, and hit Lae at 0930. The B-25's hit at 0945, and the B-26's exactly at 1000.* B-17's will go over the target at 30,000 feet the B-25's at 18,000 feet, and we'll go in at 10,000 feet. The weather is supposed to be ideal—an overcast with the top at 10,000 feet right up to Salamaua. Should be a good mission if the weather is good. Roger, Rich, and Divine worked until about 1030 on details. Now, if only those B-17's decoy the Zeros, it should be successful.

"June 8th: We sent a vehicle into town today to pick up General Ralph Royce. Got away about 1030, and brought him out here to the field. He looked over the 19th Squadron and the Headquarters area, then went down to the field to watch the ships take off. Eleven finally got away. A B-17 for

* 1000 is 1000 hours or 10:00 A.M.

General Royce was supposed to come in and take off for Port Moresby about 1400 [2 P.M.], but it never showed up. So— he's going to take off about 0300 [3 A.M.] in another B-17. Divine is going along, and will try to make this mission, but General Royce's appearance has certainly put a crimp in that. Group Commander Divine had dinner scheduled for the evening at Kennedy's—among the people there were General Royce, Colonel Perrin, and W. B. Courtney of *Collier's* Magazine, as well as some other brass."

The entry for June 9 began in this fashion:

"A *busy* day today. Colonel Divine was up at 0145 and took off into town to pick up General Royce and his party. They took off in a B-17 at 0315 for the flight to Moresby, arriving there at 0800. Navigator in the B-17 messed things up. . . ."

But there was extensive activity among the different squadrons of the 22d Bomb Group during June 8, for on this day they departed the Townsville area and staged on up to Moresby. That night they had to prepare the airplanes for the following day, checking over the bombs, the fuses, guns and ammunition supplies, survival gear, code procedures—the thousand separate little items that had to all be intermeshed into a single, smoothly functioning entity. Before they could even begin this phase of the mission, however, they first had to make that long flight across the open, shark-filled seas into Seven-Mile Drome.

During the morning of June 8 the briefings of the different squadrons "went perfectly." [44] Operations Officer Richardson had managed to obtain, by some moonlight requisitioning, a rarity in Australia: a light projector with which he flashed target maps and target close-ups on a large wall screen (a wall thoroughly whitewashed a dozen times or more).

After the briefings the pilots and their crews assembled by their planes. At each of the different fields the big engines of the Marauders coughed into life. Dust sprayed back in wind-lashed streams; beneath the huge propellers, miniature whirlwinds whipped into existence and went dancing away toward the wingtips, where they vanished in dust puffs.

Pilots played gingerly on toe brakes, the right hand of each man grasping in a loose-knuckled manner the throttle quadrants. On the rough surface beneath the planes, a sudden swerve or an unexpected stop could put a severe strain on a gear leg or wheel system—and that meant an abort. Because of the lack of parts and repairs, there were so few planes available for combat that every plane was beyond any reckoning in everyday values. Every flight up to Moresby was considered a major task, and each element of that task itself had to be played with care.

Johnson, Anderson, and Stevens were still touring the

different fields when the Marauders began the initial legs of their mission. One after the other the sleek bombers raced down the strips; one by one they blasted sand and dust and pebbles behind them, forcing the planes next in line to wait cautiously until the minor sandblast effect of the propellers had drifted from the runway.

But not even so basic a task as getting twelve airplanes off the ground on schedule—even with two days of notice and preparation—could be accomplished without its problems. Jury-rigged maintenance, parts cannibalized from any wreck lying within reach, lack of proper tools, were all factors that began to affect the mission from the very moment of its inception. The 19th Squadron remained on the ground for fifteen minutes beyond the scheduled estimated time of departure (ETD) because of difficulties in getting the fuel tanks of the Marauders fully topped off.

Then they were all off the ground. The sound of the engines vanished across the desert, and the heat pounded down and rippled the air along the horizon.

John Richardson went running out of his office when he heard the sound of engines. It was Burnside in Number 01428: he had lost all his hydraulics. The crew managed to get just enough pressure back to get the gear down. With almost a full load aboard, the B-26 came in very fast. A normal landing in the Marauder meant flying her right on down until the wheels were hugging the strip. She came over the fence indicating 130 miles per hour on the gauge, and if everything was in the groove she eased her way back to earth on the main gear at just about 120 indicated.

But with all that weight and the hot afternoon, Burnside came streaking in over the fence at better than 150 miles per hour. Everyone watching held his breath; the B-26 howled over the ground. Burnside let her roll the full length of the strip and then turned slowly onto the taxiway, gunning first one engine and then the other until he was clear of the runway. Richardson tore out to the airplane in an airdrome truck. Several minutes later, he began to curse bitterly: patched and taped together, the hydraulic system was completely shot. Marauder 01428 was out of the mission for the next day.

Not long after the first Marauder was towed to her regular position on the field, Pierre Powell came into view, nursing Number 01521. A defective generator had crippled one engine and had snarled up the electrically operated turret atop the fuselage. The crew quickly shifted their gear to another bomber—Number 01363—and in short order Powell was thundering into the air for his second take-off of the day.

Then it was Dewey Flint's turn in Marauder 01516, with the kind of trouble they had learned to expect in the 22d. The bombers were suffering from a rash of generator breakdowns, and each time that happened, the airplane systems would suffer. Sometimes the men could get away with it; most of the time, however, it meant immediate and major repair work. Richardson considered this his lucky day; the ground crews found the trouble almost at once. Less than an hour later they secured the engine cowls, and Flint and his crew were again on their way.

The twelfth Marauder—Burnside's plane—never did get off the ground. But there were some other airplanes at Moresby, and one of those was ready for flight. It would fill in the gap to bring the strength planned for the mission back to its original level.

During the afternoon of June 8, Johnson, Anderson, and Stevens met in the headquarters office of Air Commodore F. W. F. Lukis, R.A.A.F. The Australian commodore—who commanded the entire northeast sector of the continent, including Australian and American air units†—personally briefed the three officers from Washington on the many problems that could affect the mission and alter its original plans. After the briefing the three men returned to the Hotel Buchanan in Townsville.

At the hotel they met General Royce, who had arrived only that afternoon at Garbutt Field. The group of men increased in number until at the informal gathering were Johnson, Anderson, and Stevens as well as General Marquat and Colonel Connolly (base commander of Garbutt), and General Royce.[45]

War correspondents in the area (and some historical narratives many years later) have stated that MacArthur had assigned as escorts of Johnson—as well as of Anderson and Stevens—both Generals Marquat and Royce. But Ralph Royce corrects the record and states that this is absolutely false.

"The sight of the special group at the Hotel Buchanan that day," he relates, "with Colonels Anderson and Stevens, and with Commander Johnson, was a complete surprise to me. General MacArthur had never even mentioned their names to me, or that anyone from the Congress was in the area. I don't know who sent out the story that I had been designated as an escort officer to this group, because I had never heard of Johnson before, and never met him before this first time.

† Lukis is remembered as being "rather elderly and rather fat, with a big moustache, an appalling lack of knowledge of air combat operations, and a commendable honesty for admitting that he knew nothing much about airplanes except for flying boats, at which he was greatly skilled." MacArthur managed to get Lukis ousted from his post; his replacement was Major General Ralph Royce.

"It so happened that it was just at this time that I was taking over command of the Northeast Sector of Australia. I had left Melbourne on June 6 and flown up to Charleville to visit the fighter group bases in that area.

"We intended to continue on up to Port Moresby in New Guinea later on, and with the shortage of ammunition, the plane—it was a new B-17E—was loaded with ammunitions and critical supplies. We had some correspondents with us, too—Courtney of *Collier's* was there, Sherrod of *Time* Magazine, and Robinson of International News Service.

"On the morning of the seventh we flew into Townsville. I was trying to get in touch with General Brett back in Melbourne, but it was impossible—our communications weren't worth a damn. The next day, this was on the eight, I went on to Garbutt Field and had a meeting with Dwight Divine, commander of the 22d Group. We made an inspection tour of their dispersal points, their maintenance facilities, and so forth. I was trying to get a fast but a good impression of just what the situation was all about.

"We were supposed to go up to Moresby that night, the night of the eighth, and we were waiting for another B-17 to show up to carry us on. But the airplane—it was that beat-up, battered old Swoose that could barely get around—was held up by weather, and it never showed." ‡

The evening of June 8 . . .
In Townsville, at the Hotel Buchanan, Johnson, Anderson, and Stevens ate an early dinner and soon afterward retired for the night. They would be awakened shortly after 2:00 A.M. (Colonel Divine was scheduled to leave Garbutt Field at 1:45 A.M. to drive into Townsville "to pick up General Royce and his party," which included the three-man team from Washington).[46]

One hundred and eighty miles from Port Moresby, across the island of New Guinea to its northeast coast, thirty fighter pilots of the Tainan Wing gathered before a run-down shack and snapped to attention under the steely-eyed gaze of a wing officer. The time was shortly after 5:00 P.M.

The agile killers of the Lae bastion moved briskly through their gymnastic maneuvers, as was demanded by Naval Aviation Captain Masahisa Saito, Lae commander, in accordance with the stated procedures of the Imperial Navy to assure the physical fitness of pilots and to "keep our bodies agile and our reflexes sharp." [47]

After the group training, the fighter pilots on emergency

‡ Frank Kurtz, pilot of "The Swoose," had been forced down by weather conditions at Cookstown; he was unable to take off until well into the next day.

stand-by alert donned their life jackets and flight gear and moved off at double time to their Zeros. The other men returned to their billets for the evening meal. After dinner a number of them bathed or whiled away the next several hours writing letters home or reading. A few men assembled with a harmonica and an accordion and softly sang of home.

By nine o'clock that night one of the pilots blew out the candles that provided flickering illumination in a building six by ten yards. Around a center table, cots were lined along the walls. One man drew up a rolled thatched curtain to allow a breeze through the structure. Within a few minutes the only sounds were those of sleeping men.

One hundred and eighty miles from Lae, the pilots and crewmen from the twelve Marauders of the 22d Bomb Group prepared for sleep. Two men from each crew crawled into a bomber, made themselves as comfortable as it was possible to be inside the austere fuselage (it was *never* comfortable), and huddled within mosquito netting. It would be their task, should the night suddenly be split with the scream of falling bombs, to get engines started almost at once and prepare either to taxi to a dispersal point or to hazard a night take-off without lights and with cold engines.

The rest of the crew hung mosquito netting from the outer wing sections of the airplane and stretched out on the ground.

High overhead, thunder rumbled in the thick clouds, and several men stirred restlessly. It sounded unpleasantly like bombs exploding far in the distance . . .

The stage was set.

Within a matter of hours, the men sleeping in the hotel in Townsville, beneath the Marauder wings at Seven-Mile Drome, and in the shack at Lae would rendezvous high over the mountainous jungles of New Guinea.

CHAPTER TEN

THE GATHERING

The men left the briefing shack in twos and threes, dragging on cigarettes, looking impatiently at the sky, checking the time, glancing by reflex toward their waiting Marauders. It was hot and it was muggy. Thick clouds rolled across the sky over Seven-Mile, but the pilots noted that sky obscuration was decreasing; more important, there was plenty of room between the cloud bases and the mountains—room enough so that they could dismiss visions of sliding out of a mist and slamming into a mountain. It had happened.

Where was that B-17 with the VIPs? The mission was starting to fall behind schedule already . . .

"We had a normal briefing," Jerry Crosson said. "Normal for this fouled-up war, anyway. Intelligence reported that the morning report of activity at Lae and Salamaua showed some unexpected activity at Lae. Couple of transports in the harbor, with some barges. More interesting was the report that at least one, maybe two, submarines were also there. The barges were off-loading supplies to the airfield. The briefing officer said that the ships should be the primary targets rather than the airfield—but he wasn't really sure if the ships were still there. Far as we were concerned, the field was just as important—especially if we could clobber some planes on the ground or hit their fuel supply.

"Pretty much the same situation existed at Moresby—that is, the lack of any real docking facilities. They briefed us with extra caution about Lae and what was in the harbor, because our people were always worried about our getting lost in the clouds. The jungle often looks the same no matter where you are, and when you're tooling around for a while; well, if something goes wrong and you come busting out of the clouds suddenly and there's a harbor below you—it might be Moresby as well as Lae or someplace else. On June 9 we had some ships unloading with our own barges, and there was also a submarine in the harbor, and the people there were worried about the possibility, no matter how remote, that they might get clobbered by their own people. It never happened, but they always took special pains about the problem."

The men kept glancing at their watches and at the clouds and at the sky toward Australia; they were starting to become fidgety. It was not only the matter of coordinating this mission with the other planes. There was also the wind and the temperature and the poor runway, and every pilot in his own mind could see the margin between a safe and a critical take-off getting smaller and smaller.

"You made your take-offs either downhill or uphill—simple as that," John Ewbank (who led the second wave) said slowly. "When we took off uphill we had to face that range of hills between the end of the runway and the ocean. It sure made for some moments of—let's call it an adventure. You'd take off, kind of working your way down a valley, and with a really full load you'd stagger along and you had to haul yourself up and over those hills. The trouble was, you couldn't even turn to get into a better position. Either way that you turned you were turning toward, into, some more hills. And so you tried to keep going down that valley as long as possible, building up speed and lift and grabbing for enough altitude to get over the hills."

Earlier that same day, while it was still pitch-black at Garbutt Field, several old staff cars, coated with dust and creaking badly from battered springs, drove across a runway. Armed sentries wearing Australian and American uniforms watched the cars come to a stop near a hulking form alongside a taxiway. Car doors opened and slammed shut, and voices drifted in a jumble across the flat expanse.

Figures began to climb into a new B-17E bomber. After the last hatch slammed shut, the staff cars drove off in their rush to be clear of the airplane.

The pilot slid back the side window of the big bomber, stuck his head through, and glanced at the shadowy form of a ground crewman. A dull light rotated. The pilot turned to the man at his right. Together, hands moving to the switch console between them and to another bank of controls above their heads, they fed electrical energy to the engines. Several minutes later, all four engines thundered and the bomber moved carefully from its parking stand. Each time the pilot pushed down on the rudder pedals to work the brakes, a generator behind and below the copilot's seat whined in frenzy.

The sound carried back through the airplane, past the bomb bay and the narrow catwalk, into the fuselage. The floor of the airplane rose at a steep angle, higher toward the nose. A jumble of life rafts, spare parts, machine guns, ammunition, and bodies shook and bounced as the bomber trundled toward the end of the runway.

Men shifted their positions to seek comfort. For several minutes there was a deafening roar as the pilots checked out each engine at full power, swung around to the runway, and started the Flying Fortress on its way. The vibration eased as the big wheels lifted from the dirt and rose into their retraction bays.

Lyndon Johnson sprawled out across a life raft. Sam Anderson and Francis Stevens pushed their bodies against parachutes as they settled down to grab an hour or more of sleep. Other men tried to gain comfort along the curving belly of the airplane.[48]

The noise quieted down to a numbing drone as the bomber sped on toward the dawn. During the flight the pilot asked his navigator for a position report. The answer was long in coming, and finally the embarrassed officer reported to his pilot that he did not *know* where they were, not for certain, anyway . . .

The first phase of the all-important coordinated air strike was rapidly going awry.

At Seven-Mile Drome, the grumbling pilots who cursed the delay were being told to wait until the brass arrived. Brigadier General Martin F. Scanlon checked the time and, without realizing the gesture, glanced skyward for some sign of the expected bomber with its special load of passengers. There had been a rash of visiting firemen coming in to Moresby in recent weeks.[49] Many of them had tasks to carry out in the harbor, at the airfield, and even inland through the jungle, closer toward the Japanese troops who were entertaining ideas of driving straight across New Guinea to the American-Australian air base and port. Engineers had come to build fortifications, better harbor facilities, new airstrips. On June 7 there had come perhaps the most unusual of Scanlon's visitors: three Navaho Indians who showed up unexpectedly at Seven-Mile. The Navahos were invaluable; close to the Japanese lines they conducted all message transmissions for the Allied forces in the Navaho tongue. Japanese experts who intercepted these messages went wild trying to determine just what was going on.

The day after the Navahos arrived, Mike Scanlon received a "hot message" from Australia that on the morning of the ninth, a group of observers would arrive at Seven-Mile to fly the mission then scheduled against Lae.

"The signal we received," explained Mike Scanlon, "emphasized strongly that an important Congressman would be arriving on the morning following. No question but that the message came, or at least that it originated, from the headquarters in Melbourne of General MacArthur.

It seems beyond question that, until MacArthur's staff passed on the word that the lieutenant commander was also an "important Congressman," Lyndon Johnson had not been openly identified in this capacity. Ralph Royce had long held the reputation of being singularly unimpressed with visiting dignitaries; unless he believed they were present for a specific and worthwhile purpose, this blunt-speaking general officer, who had an outstanding combat record in two wars, would ignore a VIP no matter what his status. The idea that Royce personally, as the newly appointed commander of air units in northeast Australia and New Guinea, would go to the trouble of alerting Scanlon or anyone else about an "important Congressman" was completely at variance with Royce's actions and reputation. And as he himself stated, General Royce never knew of Johnson's being in the area until he met him personally in Townsville.

"I met Commander Johnson and General Royce when they landed at Seven-Mile," Scanlon added. "They flew in with a B-17 in the morning with a fairly large number of people. Dwight Divine, who commanded the 22d Bomb Group, was also on that plane, and I arranged with Dwight to have three of the people go along with the B-26's that were going to hit Lae.

"We hadn't had a raid against Lae for a while, and I was planning to make the mission myself, as I'd done with different types of planes against the various targets we were hitting, all the way up to Rabaul.* Several other people also wanted to go, but there just weren't enough planes with space or parachutes enough to accommodate them all." [50]

The description of Lyndon Johnson early that morning—as recorded in the notes written by Mike Scanlon in the days following the mission—provide the viewpoint of a man noted for his keen observations of people. Mike Scanlon while still at Moresby wrote in his personal papers that

"The message we had received about the 'very important Congressman' was pretty formal. He was an affable, nice person in the uniform of a lieutenant commander, who was doing a job and making very little fuss about it. He was the first Congressman who ever showed up at Moresby, where we were getting plenty of attention from the Japanese, who used to bomb us at least two or three nights a week, plus day raids and strafing attacks by Zeros that would shoot anything that moved at our base."

At Seven-Mile Drome, the pilots continued to wait for the VIPs to appear. The scheduled take-off time arrived, and the airplanes still stood off the runway, engines and propellers silent. The only movement among the crews was the impatient pacing and the angry gestures of the pilots. Four miles away, at Three-Mile Drome, the decoy bombers—a small group of B-25s—still awaited the signal to take off. But every man among the Marauders at Seven-Mile knew that the three B-17 heavy bombers scheduled to strike first at Lae were already in the air, and that the initial phase of the mission was under way.† With every passing minute, the opportunity to draw off the Zero fighters protecting Lae, to catch them with fuel tanks low or even empty, was disappearing.

"The operations people at Seven-Mile kept telling us to wait, to keep holding up the scheduled take-off time for the strike," Walter Krell explained. "Yet, dammit, everything had been worked out so carefully that the least break in the

* Brigadier General Mike Scanlon had, in fact, "frightened the wits" out of a B-25 crewman during an attack against Lae. Determined to see exactly what was happening, Scanlon grasped a structural member, straddled the open bomb bay with his feet, and looked straight down to watch the plane's bombs hurtling earthward. He said after the mission that he was "quite satisfied with the view."

† The pilots of the B-26 bombers waiting at Seven-Mile were unaware that the 19th Bomb Group was able to get only two B-17s into the air instead of the three bombers scheduled.

schedule we'd planned could let everything start coming un-glued at the seams. I was more than a little miffed about this; and this involved more than just timing our bomb run with the flights of the B-17s and the B-25s. We had that uphill-downhill runway to worry about, and if conditions weren't prime, things could get pretty hairy.

"Above all, we didn't want any part of the uphill take-off if we could help it, especially with the load we were carrying in those planes. Some of us were carrying four 1000-pounders, and that's a great load for the B-26; other ships were just about bulging with 100-pounders to crater the Lae runways. The point was that it's always better to be making the take-off roll downhill.

"But if we were kept waiting on the ground until it became 0815 or 0820, or a little later . . . well, that's when things started to get hairy. You could look at the windsock and you just knew that about this time of the morning the thing would start to pick up and the wind would start to shift on us. If we went uphill we would be working every inch of the way.

"Then, of course, we would have to flog the engines so we could work our way up through the valley. The airplanes could hack it, all right, because we had already done it so many times that it was a matter of repeating past perform-ances. But no one likes to do a take-off and climb-out at maximum gross—and some of us were even overloaded. There was that mushy runway to consider, the minimum clearance of eight or nine inches between the props and the surface, the rocks that were picked up that would nick the blades and slam like bullets against the fuselage; you could hear them banging away and they scared hell out of you.

"Anyway, I was getting more annoyed by the whole thing. We waited and we waited, and the wind was shifting right in front of us and the temperature was going up, and I finally got so fed up with the way the time was just going that—well, I'd had it.

"I told the guys we would give them just about another five minutes and then to blazes with 'em; we were going whether that plane came in or not. If the brass wanted to come along, let them show up on time. The Japanese sure weren't going to cooperate.

"Well, there were guys running back and forth in jeeps between our planes and the operations shack. They kept tell-ing us to quiet down and to wait, and I read them off good and proper. It must have been the beginning of a grand flap, because finally one guy came tearing over in a jeep and told us the general had given a direct order that we weren't to leave, to take off, without his specific permission. It was a great way to fight a war.

"Finally, about three or four minutes after I'd said we were going 'no matter what,' this B-17 came in. Out poured all the rank. By some strange touch of good luck, that B-17 pilot didn't park at the other end of the field, but pretty close to us.

"Sam Anderson latched on to us right away, as we had expected. I looked at him and asked him where he'd been. Sam grinned at me and climbed aboard. . . ."

CHAPTER ELEVEN

FATE

Lyndon Johnson climbed down from the four-engined heavy bomber onto the dusty taxiway of Seven-Mile Drome. Ahead and to the left of the B-17E that had brought him to New Guinea was another Flying Fortress. To the right stood the line of Marauders from the 22d Bomb Group.

Several trucks and staff cars in fading olive-drab paint drove up to the airplane as the remaining passengers and crew from the bomber assembled in a group. Over his lightweight chino * shirt and black tie Johnson still wore a dark jacket; it had been cold in the airplane. General Royce stood by, along with several officers, as Johnson relaxed, leaning against the grillwork of a staff car.

General Scanlon drove up moments later—dressed as always in his Australian uniform of short tropical pants, Scanlon's formula for comfort in the steaming Moresby area. He greeted Johnson warmly. For the next several minutes Johnson, Royce, and Scanlon discussed the mission (Dwight Divine had already spoken to Scanlon about arrangements for the Washington trio to join the Marauder crews).

They assigned Johnson to fly with Lieutenant Willis G. Bench of Headquarters Squadron. Johnson looked at the painting of a dumpy cartoon figure painted on the side of the nose and the name "Wabash Cannonball" † above the figure. He was introduced to the crew, and then one of the men led Johnson into the airplane. Six feet two inches in height, Johnson found the going cramped. He climbed into the narrow cubicle behind the cockpit and directly against the bulkhead

* Khakis or suntans.
† Martin B-26 Marauder Number 01508.

that separated the cubicle from the bomb bay. A moment later, Johnson emerged from the bomber. There was still a delay in the take-off, and he walked away from the B-26 for a minute or two.‡

When he started to get back into the airplane, he was surprised to find "Steve"—Francis Stevens—occupying the seat. Despite the fact that Johnson said he'd been aboard the "Wabash Cannonball" first, Stevens only grinned and refused to give up the seat, telling his friend that he would just have to find another airplane in which to fly.[51]

Johnson finally shrugged and walked off to find another plane. As Lieutenant Walter H. Greer stood outside the "Heckling Hare" § with his crew, Johnson approached them and said, "I'd like to fly with you, Captain Greer."

"Arkie" Greer shook hands with the lieutenant commander‖ and said quietly, "Fine. Sure, you can go." Greer motioned for his copilot, Australian Flight Sergeant G. A. McMullin, to come up and meet their "guest" for the mission.[52]

The "Heckling Hare" was also known to the crew as the "Arkansas Traveler," bestowed in deference to the succession of airplanes Greer had flown. A landing accident back in the States had finished off the first "Arkansas Traveler." A Japanese bomb exploding right on target at Moresby attended to the second bomber (Serial Number 01429). On the left side of the fuselage beneath the pilot's window, there was painted the caricature of the "Heckling Hare"—a knobby-jointed rabbit reclining on a flying carpet and idly dropping bombs over the side.

Johnson turned to the group of men who made up the rest of the crew and asked them directly if they would mind his going along on the mission.

Corporal Harry G. Baren, a huge six-foot-tall man who manned the tail gun of the B-26, looked up at the Navy officer. "Heck, no," he smiled. "C'mon along if you want."

The rest of the men nodded their assent, and Johnson introduced himself, saying that he was from Texas. This brought immediate smiles from the crew; several of them were from the South.

‡ The authors were unable to learn the reason for Commander Johnson's leaving the plane.

§ Martin B-26 Marauder Number 01488. Originally, it was believed that this was a B-26A model, but this report has been proved incorrect; the authors have studied the 19th Squadron records of each aircraft to confirm this point.

‖ Conversations with members of the 22d Bomb Group, and notably with surviving members of Greer's crew, establish conclusively that none of these men were aware that Johnson was (1) a Congressman or (2) on a mission as a special representative of President Roosevelt.

"Johnson at that time was thin," recalled Sergeant Claude A. McCredie. "In fact, one of the crew referred to him as a 'long, skinny boy from the South.' I asked him if he would like to take a look in the bay and see the bombs. We were getting them fused and ready for the mission at the moment— one of the last things we do before climbing aboard and starting to taxi out. He showed close interest in what we were doing. In fact, I was startled at the questions he asked me. We've had the 'wheels' that came poking around before, but it was more for effect than anything else. You can tell at once if a man really is interested or if he's just acting to put on a show. Most of that type would never dream of going along on a combat mission—not against Lae, especially. Down there at the time, the word 'Lae' was almost synonymous with hell, and the odds were about one in four or five that you wouldn't make it back from the mission."

"At first we didn't pay very much attention to this guy in a Navy uniform," explained Harry Baren. "When we were preparing for the mission we weren't interested in meeting people, and we couldn't have cared less about who they were. We had a mission to fly, we had to get ready for it, and that meant revving up the engines, checking out the guns, being extra careful with the bombs, going over the instruments and the fuel system and a lot of other things. When you're attending to all the things that add up to your return ticket home from Lae, you're a fool if you don't watch everything you do. We had a really great crew, and everyone was right on the ball."

Johnson watched the crew attending to their work. He walked up to Baren. "What's your name, Corporal?" he asked.

"We started to kibitz around," Baren said. "The moment you started talking with him, you liked the guy. There wasn't any mistaking his interest; you get a sixth sense about that. Then we started kidding him. I said to him: 'Commander, what are you doing here, anyway? We don't need the Navy to help us out.'

"He laughed at me, and explained he was on an inspection mission to see just what conditions were like in the area. One thing led to another and we began to talk about the mission we were about to fly. It suddenly dawned on me that this guy was really coming along to Lae with us.

"He must have been crazy; I told him that. We had pilots and crewmen who had made a few missions and then flat refused to fly over Lae or Rabaul any more; they couldn't have cared less if they were court-martialed or not. To them, Lae especially was suicide. They figured you could never survive more than a few missions over *that* target. And here was this tall, thin fella who didn't have to go, and he was asking to come along and get his head shot off."

"Harry Baren always was one for spitting right out whatever he had inside him," McCredie recalled with a laugh. "He called a spade a spade. We were real fond of him; he could really play a tune with that big fifty-caliber tail gun of his. He cocked his head and looked at Johnson, and then he seemed to take a real liking to Johnson, because he tried to talk him out of the mission."

Baren did exactly that, but not in the same terms that Marquat had used. He looked Johnson straight in the eye.

"Commander, let me give you some advice," he began. "This ain't no milk run, believe me! You don't need to come along and get shot up to find out about conditions here, or the things we need; we'll *tell* you that. If you're smart, Commander, you'll stay right here on the ground. You can get all the reports you want right from the operations tent—just like all the other people who come up here."

Johnson broke in and explained to Baren that he had come here to find out for himself just what was going on in the theater. "He said to me," Baren related, "that the only way a man could ever know what things were like was to go out and see it with his own eyes, and to experience it for himself. He sure didn't go much for secondhand information; he was absolutely determined to get on that mission with us.

"Well—after all that, and with what else I knew he had already learned about the situation over Lae, this man just had to have guts. I gave it a whirl again. I told him just how rough it was up there and he was going to get shot up, and all he did was grin. He said there was only one way to find out if I was really talking with inside information.

"So I dropped the subject, and took off on his uniform. I said to him, 'How come you're wearing that Navy suit?' He swung right into the feeling of things and began to joke with us like he was one of the crew. He explained that he couldn't go around without a uniform—because if he were shot down with us his uniform would protect him as a prisoner of war. We were kibitzing around some more, and then the Southern boys in the crew joined in.

"They were really enjoying themselves—and so was he. They'd heard me giving him the works on what it was like over Lae—but you can't exaggerate what things were like up there; it's just impossible—so they picked up this bit about his being from the South. They were real proud he was a Southerner. They said we've got the best pilot in the business, and he's from down Arkansas, and that he—Johnson—naturally *must* be from the South. Texas made it something special, the boys said, and Johnson looked real proud to be accepted so completely by the crew."

"That's a point well taken," McCredie said. "It's difficult to realize just how close we were on those planes. Not only from trusting our lives to each other in a fight, but also because we were fighting the toughest odds in the Pacific. We were also convinced that they'd sort of given us up back in the States, and that brings you even closer. And here's this Navy fellow, and he's a real human being, and he's honestly interested in what we're doing—we can spot the phony twenty miles off. But every man in that crew really accepted Johnson. There's nothing halfway about something like this. You're either all the way in with the crew, or they'll tell you right smack to your face to buzz off.

"Johnson got serious all of a sudden. He told us carefully that his job was to find out just what our problems were, that he was here to help as much as he could.

"Then he asked us if we had any complaints. Well, all you had to do was to ask Harry Baren, and he came right back at you and answered you with the unvarnished truth."

When Johnson asked if the crew had a specific matter on which there could be improvement, Harry Baren cracked, "Sure there is, Commander. Get us some fighters out here. It would be a pleasure for those Zeros to have somebody to worry about, instead of our worrying about them. Fighters—that's what we need. Fighters that can go all the way with us over the target, and let us really get those bombs in where they belong."

Johnson then brought up the matter of shortages in parts and supplies. Baren grinned. "Listen, Commander, it's probably not as bad as you've heard," he replied. "It's at least twice as bad as anything you've heard."

They discussed things in general—combat conditions, tactics, the enemy—and Lyndon Johnson probably received much more candor from Harry Baren than he may have expected. Baren had some strong thoughts # and he did not hold them back.

"I told Johnson," Baren related, "that we couldn't have cared less what the papers were saying about MacArthur back in the States. Out here, where the chips were down, he was probably the most unpopular man we knew of.

"I said then—and I stand on what I said—that we felt a lot of our people were being killed without any real reason. Our intelligence wasn't worth a damn. It really wasn't; the only intelligence we ever had that amounted to a row of beans came out when the crews got together after a mission. We'd meet in the operations tent and add up together what we had all seen individually, and from that we had some sort of a

And he still does, it should be noted. Baren's convictions on these matters have not been altered by the years.

picture with reality to it. The crews on one mission would warn the next crews to go out where the flak guns had been moved to, where they could expect fighters, and what problems they might expect. That was about the *only* intelligence we had. All we ever knew about MacArthur were his fancy press pictures and his statements about the war. We'd read official communiqués that went back to the States about smashing air attacks and how many Zeros were shot down and so forth. Well, if we ever shot down as many planes as his headquarters used to say—we'd have wiped out the Jap Air Force in two months."

Baren was really warming to the subject when Greer called for the men to prepare to board the plane. Johnson and the tailgunner walked together to the Marauder, and Johnson at that moment asked if there was an extra parachute aboard the B-26 for him.

"Parachute? Just what do you want with a parachute, Commander?" asked Baren.

Johnson stopped for a moment and looked at Baren. The tailgunner laughed and explained that "If we get hit you're not gonna need a parachute—you're gonna need a shovel to dig your way out of the hole we'll make when we auger in." [52]

Johnson laughed with him. What he did not realize was that the parachute he was about to put on belonged to Harry Baren. There was no extra parachute in the plane and Baren flew the entire mission without one.

One of the men explained that the general's orders were clear: Johnson and the other observers were to wear parachutes. Baren and another gunner helped Johnson on with the harness; Johnson was taller by several inches than any of the crew. Since several of the bombers were already running up their engines, there was no time left to adjust the chute harness for comfort. The straps pulled tightly, and Johnson had to fly the mission unable to stand erect. That did not matter much in the B-26, of course, because there was no room for a man of Johnson's height to stand up completely straight.

Several minutes later, all the men were aboard and the Marauder eased slowly from its parking space onto the taxiway. Lyndon Johnson sat in the small compartment that normally housed the navigator and the radio operator; he was on the right—or radioman's side—with a seat belt on during the take-off.

It is not much of a compartment. Two small steps lead down from the cockpit into a narrow, constricted passageway. Where the passageway broadens out on either side, there is on the right the radio equipment and on the left a seat and small desk for the navigator. Lieutenant Billy B. Boothe was the navigator for the "Heckling Hare," and Corporal Lillis M. Walker the radioman-gunner.

Walker moved back toward the two lower waist guns near the tail during the take-off. Once in the air, Johnson would be able to slide over to the left side of the fuselage, where he could look out a small window. Above him was a clear Plexiglas bubble dome through which he could look across the top of the airplane and observe clearly the entire sky above and the planes of the different formations.

Little did he dream that, slightly more than one hour after the Marauders roared into the air from Seven-Mile Drome, one bomber would be torn apart by a Japanese fighter, to reel from the sky, faster and faster, and smash into the ocean, exploding and disintegrating upon impact. The name of that airplane: "Wabash Cannonball."

CHAPTER TWELVE

THE MISSION

The first Marauder taxied to the end of the runway and swung around, rocking gently up and down on its nose gear as the pilots' feet pushed down on the toe brakes. Walt Krell and his copilot, R.A.A.F. Flight Sergeant Graham Robertson, quickly ran the bomber to take-off power.

Krell's right hand smoothly moved the twin throttles forward; Robertson checked the mixture at full rich. The huge propeller blades twisted to come around to flat pitch for maximum revolutions; engine cowl flaps moved to one-quarter open; wing flaps slid down to the quarter position.

Quickly the two men scanned the dials and gauges in the cockpit, checked the propellers at 3200 revolutions per minute (rpm). They nodded in satisfaction: both engines were pulling 35 inches of manifold pressure.

Both men suddenly rotated their feet to release their toe pressure on the brakes. Instantly, the Marauder grabbed at the air with her thrashing blades, bursting ahead with acceleration great enough to shove the pilots' bodies against their seats.

Faster and faster the plane moved down the runway, tires slicing through the soft, treacherous surface. Twelve hundred feet from their starting point, Krell eased back ever so gently on the control yoke while Robertson kept scanning the instruments. Krell brought the nose wheel off the runway, reduced the drag of the nose wheel, and changed the angle at which the wings sliced through the air, again increasing the lift produced by the short, sleek airfoils stretching out on either side of the airplane.

He played the Marauder like the thoroughbred she was. He did not haul her crudely off the ground; he let her pound faster and faster, the end of the runway rushing toward them, until, with the wings working now as they should and lift shoving hard against gravity, she flew herself away from the earth and slid into flight.

As Krell snapped, *"Gear UP!"* Robertson hit the gear lever, and the tricycle gear began pulling upward into its different wells; door covers snapped shut to present a sleek and stream-lined shape to the wind. Eight hundred feet higher than the take-off point, Robertson "milked up" the flaps, bringing them slowly into the wings. Krell eased back on the power to 3000 rpm and 32 inches manifold pressure. He closed the cowl flaps until the engine shapes, too, were almost perfectly clean.

Krell and Robertson grinned; one more take-off out of the way, and the "Kansas Comet" grabbing for sky. Sam Anderson stuck his head between them to look forward.

Behind them, Robert Hatch was thundering down the runway, mixing the swirling dust of his own take-off with that drifting from the movement of Krell's plane; then came Al Stanwood, rolling along in "Pistol Packin' Momma" and, hard on his heels, Pierre Powell in the fourth and last ship of the lead formation. Dwight Divine was in this airplane.

The 19th Squadron was in the air.

The second group of four began to roll. Johnny Ewbank rammed "Old Timer" down the runway through the dust, with Otto McIver pounding down the strip right behind him. Next came Jerry Crosson in "So Sorry." The fourth plane of the second wave was the "Wabash Cannonball"—Willis Bench and R.A.A.F. Pilot Officer L. Passmore at the controls and Francis Stevens in the radio compartment as observer.

One by one the airplanes in the third wave began rolling: Dewey Flint in "Calamity Jane," Fred Nichols in the "Flying Parson," Walt Greer and McMullin—and Lyndon Johnson—in the "Heckling Hare." Twelfth and bringing up the tail of the striking force were Howard Hayes and the fourth Australian copilot on the mission: Flight Sergeant Jimmy Reed. The "Shamrock" hurled her thunder at the jungle, and silence began to creep back into Seven-Mile. The men on the ground looked at the sky where the sleek shapes wheeled smoothly and began to come close together in flight. They would share the comfort and protection of cross fire from the six machine guns in each bomber, and they would be able to communicate through wing signals; strict radio silence was mandatory to avoid letting the enemy know that company was on its way.

"The sky that morning was pretty well overcast," recalled

Jerry Crosson. "The take-off, with all that followed, stamped this mission indelibly in my mind. We climbed on up through the overcast and then dragged our way over it. Then, finally, with everyone in sight and the formations coming in tighter—but not yet in the tight setup we would have for the combat area—we kept climbing over the Owen Stanley Range. Then we were at fourteen thousand feet and in level flight, and it was always a bit rough at this height, even for a short period, because we didn't have any oxygen in the airplanes. Once we leveled off, we began to pick up our speed. It came slowly because with all our weight aboard we were near the top altitude of the airplanes, and the speed has to be squeezed out when everything is so close to its maximum.

"Finally we were working our way along in the groove; we were approaching the target and I was trying to watch Johnny Ewbank ahead and off to one side, and also stay locked tight in formation with him; and at the same time I sure had one eyeball roving around looking for the B-25s which were to decoy those Zeros away from Lae, and let us get in nice and neat and clobber them good. I was really looking forward to that. . . ."

Every mission in its over-all scene is pretty much the same to the pilots of different planes, but the smaller details and the points of view always vary, because the perspective is different and location in a formation can sometimes mean everything. At the forefront of the formation of three rows of bombers—each row a staggered *V* shape—Walt Krell pushed the "Kansas Comet" along on its course. "We came along over the Owen Stanleys, still in a climbing attitude," he said, "preparing to swing off to our right to Lae, and getting set up to begin the bomb run.

"Powell was behind me and he just wouldn't hold his position in tight; he kept falling back. I kept radio silence, but I flipped my wings, and that was the unmistakable signal to get in *real* tight. I don't know what was the matter with him, but he wouldn't tuck it in . . ."

Johnny Ewbank, leading the second wave, said: "We took a different route than we usually followed for our attacks against the Lae area. This was the first time we went more to the west and further north, working our way over the Markham Valley before coming around to take a whack at the target. The hills were high along this route. We were looking forward to this mission, really looking forward to it. The whole plan sounded great to us, and if the B-17 decoys and then the second attack by the few B-25s worked out according to plan, we would slam into Lae when they were really helpless. We wanted a time lag of thirty to forty minutes between the B-17s and our strike. This meant the Zeros would just have landed at Lae, and we'd hit them hard and fast while they were still trying to refuel their planes. We thought about all this and we were actually grinning over the prospects of *this* strike. We had everything set to do some real precision bombing from ten thousand feet.

"We came around the mountains well above our bombing altitude and then prepared for a gradual descent once clear of the peaks. We would pick up speed in our descent and set up the bombing run just the way we wanted it. Then I saw Lae off to our left. And Salamaua was really clear beyond the clouds. The weather had broken perfectly and I saw the little peninsula of Salamaua sticking out in the water. Lae was easy to spot in its cove, by the river running up through the valley, and we spotted both of them.

"But what I saw next just froze in my mind. . . ."

At Lae it was suddenly a beautiful morning. The storm clouds had broken, and sunshine streamed down onto the field. Naval Aviation Captain Masahisa Saito, one of the keenest minds in the Imperial Navy, looked upward at the sky. The day promised action, he thought. He discussed the possibility with his immediate subordinate, Commander Tadachi Nakajima; there had been no attacks against Lae for at least four days, and the changing pattern of the weather was ideal for concealing the movement of bomber formations until they should burst from the clouds and attack. Saito and Nakajima studied the scene on the field. Twenty-five Zero fighters were at the ready.[53]

Alongside the runway, the fighter pilots did not really believe there would be an attack. The commander might believe otherwise, but with this weather . . . ? The men on interceptor alert relaxed, laughing and joking among themselves. There was much conversation on the field because of the presence of Hajima Yoshida. The war correspondent-photographer for the newspaper *Yomiuri* had come down from Rabaul to take pictures for people back home in Japan. They were anxious to see photographs of their most famous pilots: the great aces of the Tainan Wing. Yoshida busied himself happily (and used a timer to include himself in several pictures as well, with a flier's helmet and goggles perched atop his head), for he was having a fabulous morning. Among the great aces, and the pilot newcomers at Lae, he had captured on film Sakai, Sasai, Yonekawa, Nishizawa, Ota, Endo, Takatsuka, Handa, Hatori, Yamashita, Ishikawa, Kikuchi, Yoshino, Nakajima, Uehara, Yamazaki, Oki, Miya, Motoyoshi, and still others.

Hajima Yoshida was especially delighted with the pictures he had been able to take of Saburo Sakai, Hiroyoshi Nishizawa, and Toshio Ota, the three pilots who were at that time Japan's leading aces. And to have them all together! It was a wonderful opportunity. With the war barely seven months old, the three aces had already shot down a total of more than sixty or seventy enemy planes.

They were known in the Japanese Navy as the "Cleanup Trio" because of their spectacular success when operating as a team. They were also known, but not by name, to the men of Seven-Mile Drome at Moresby. For these were the same three pilots who had slipped away from their formations after an escort mission against Moresby and raced back to the airfield. Several thousand feet above the startled Americans and Australians on the ground, the trio had slipped into perfect wingtip-to-wingtip formation and performed a series of beautifully executed precision loops, one after the other, in a bizarre invitation to the Americans and Australians to come up and fight.

Later that same night—May 17—a lone American bomber had thundered low over the Lae airstrip. An object plummeted earthward but failed to explode. The surprised Japanese rushed the container into the hands of Lieutenant Junichi Sasai. Within that container was a message from the fighter pilots of Seven-Mile Drome:

To the Lae Commander: We were much impressed with those three pilots who visited us today, and we all liked the loops they flew over our field. It was quite an exhibition. We would appreciate it if these same pilots returned here once again, each wearing a green muffler around his neck. We're sorry we couldn't give them better attention on their last trip, but we will see to it that next time they will receive an all-out welcome from us.

Even as the American formations roared toward Lae, Yoshida was completing his photographic work. He particularly wanted to get seven pilots, among them Saburo Sakai, in a special group portrait (including, of course, Yoshida). The inclusion of Sakai in this group was to be of profound importance before the day was over.

The heavy cloud cover broke swiftly and brought sunlight streaming down even more brightly than before and Yoshida hurried to take advantage of his good fortune. His camera on a tripod, Yoshida set the timer and hurried forward to join the group of seven pilots standing near the tail of a Zero. He placed his left hand jauntily on his hip and stared at the lens; the shutter clicked.

The camera had just snapped when—exactly at 8:40 A.M.—the Navy gunners manning the antiaircraft batteries along the strip started shouting, *"Enemy planes! Alert! Alert!"* Discordant noise shattered the quiet morning. Buckets, drums, hollow logs, and the like were hammered mightily to sound the warning, and two buglers blew furiously to complete the din of the scramble alert.

"Because we were taking this particular photograph," explained Yoshida, "Saburo Sakai and the other pilots in this group were some distance from their fighters. Consequently, they were delayed in the wild scramble, and they took off behind the other fighters. As a result they were unable to press home their attacks against the B-25s—which were already being hit by the eighteen other Zeros which took off before them. Ironically, it was this very delay in the pursuit of the Mitchell bombers that enabled Sakai and his men to be the first pilots to attack the Marauders."

The official Japanese combat log of the day, kept by Captain Saito, shows that from 8:45 A.M. through 9:30 A.M. on June 9, twenty-five Zero fighters engaged the enemy over an area extending from Salamaua to Cape Ward Hunt. . . .

There is always one very special point of view in any battle—that of the enemy. Here is Saburo Sakai's description of the opening phases of the air battle on June 9, 1942.*

"No sooner had the camera shutter clicked than the air raid alarms burst forth from the command post," relates Sakai. "Within seconds the entire base erupted into a hornet's nest. Every pilot on alert duty ran as fast as he could to the Zero fighters parked on each side of the runway. There was no plan, no purpose worked out for the interception. It was a wild scramble, a matter of first come, first fly. Whoever could clamber first into a Zero cockpit immediately fired up his engine and began taxiing. What made matters even more confused—and dangerous!—was the fact that we had so many of the green pilots, newly arrived at the base, ready to scramble. These were the men who still had to be weaned in battle. Not yet permitted to fly long-range escort or sweep missions, they regarded a scramble as their own personal opportunity to wage war against the enemy. It was wild exuberance.

"Even before I could get to a fighter, three rookie pilots in the group of seven posing for the photograph dashed madly away and almost threw themselves into the cockpits of nearby fighters. I cursed my own stupidity for not being near my own plane or ordering a Zero held specifically for me in the event of an alert. I was running past the command post, my life jacket restricting my movement, when I heard Commander Nakajima shouting at me above the roar of engines. "Sakai! There are two B-17s! Very high!" I waved my hand to indicate I had heard his message, and continued running.

"I managed to reach what appeared to be the last available

* Of the twenty-five Zero pilots who engaged in the air battle that day, Saburo Sakai is the only man to survive the war. He was Japan's greatest living ace, with 64 kills in aerial combat officially confirmed by government records.

plane parked on the southern side of the airstrip—the second strip that paralleled the main runway to the north. Normally, we made our take-offs toward the sea, giving us plenty of room to build up speed after getting the gear retracted. It was possible in the Zero to take off at just about stalling speed, and then to accelerate very rapidly once you became airborne. But today there wasn't the slightest chance for a seaward take-off; I was already too close to the water. I fired up the engine and jumped the brakes; the Zero swung obediently onto the runway. Still turning, I pushed the throttle forward to maximum power. The fighter accelerated swiftly and I began to ease back on the stick.

"My heart froze. Coming straight down the same runway at breakneck spead, directly toward me, was another Zero fighter! A head-on collision seemed inevitable as the two airplanes rushed closer with increasing speed. I didn't think; acting by reflex only, I jerked the stick hard over to the left and tramped right rudder. The Zero skidded wildly even as its wheels broke from the runway. I will swear the other airplane roared past me with less than a foot's clearance between our two fighters.

"I had barely gotten into the air, and I could already feel the cold sweat pouring down my back. The next moment my fear was gone, replaced with a mounting rage.

"Never in all my experience had I known a worse mess. There simply was no order, no plan. It is a miracle that we did not have several collisions among the Zeros.

"Somehow, we all managed to get into the air without any wreckage spilling back down on the field. We were hardly airborne when several of us (we discussed this later that day) apparently at the same moment sighted five B-25 bombers racing toward Salamaua. Every one of the twenty-five pilots in the Zeros was under full war emergency power, climbing with all the speed we could squeeze from the fighters. I dismissed the B-17s from my thoughts; obviously they were flying very high, well above the clouds. None of the other pilots recalled seeing the two bombers, although they were spotted from the ground by antiaircraft crews.

"There was no question in my own mind that the pilots of the enemy bombers were caught completely by surprise at our appearance. Once we were in sight of them, the five Mitchells salvoed their bombs toward Salamaua (damage was negligible; most of the bombs fell wide of the substation). Every Zero in the air raced after them at full speed.

"I brought the engine to overboost and gradually began to close the distance between myself and the Zeros that had first taken off. Ahead of me, the lead fighters were closing within firing range of the B-25s. I found myself cursing aloud in the cockpit with no one to hear my voice except myself.

"There were simply too many Zeros in the air to carry out an effective attack against the five enemy planes! The rookie pilots had thrown all their training to the wind and were hurling their airplanes in wild abandon at the enemy. It wasn't a pursuit; it turned into a wild free-for-all, with Zeros rushing in against the bombers from all directions. With the near-collision of the take-off still so fresh in my mind, I stared numbly at the swirling planes ahead of me, expecting at any moment to see Zeros colliding.

"Finally I was within firing range of the last American bomber, and I swung in for a firing pass. I managed to squeeze out a burst with the two nose guns from about two hundred yards' range. I was certain that I had definitely hit the airplane, but it flew on without any sign of damage.

"I broke to the left in a climbing turn and looked behind me—an instinctive reflex that has more than once kept me alive in a fight. In the distance I saw a group of specks. Just as I had thought: fighters coming in to hit us while we were occupied by the bombers. But . . . I concentrated on the group of specks. They were bombers! And they were rushing directly toward Lae! The five Mitchells were a decoy—and we had fallen right in with the plans of the enemy . . .

"Furious at myself for not anticipating such a move, I came around in a tight turn, cutting in by several Zeros; I rocked the wings violently and pointed. At once seven Zeros swung in behind me to follow me back toward Lae. By now I could make out the enemy planes—twelve Marauders coming almost head-on toward me.

"With the engine on overboost and the distance between the Zeros and the Marauders closing swiftly, I selected my targets. The bombers on the right. . . . I watched the formations close together, tightening up, nose guns and turrets already winking brilliantly, the tracers drifting toward our planes. All right then! We shall see what happens. I dropped the nose to pick up more speed . . ."

CHAPTER THIRTEEN

COMBAT

As seen from the lead bomber, "Kansas Comet"; the pilot Walt Krell . . .

"When I saw all those Zeros piling up above those cumulous clouds, I couldn't figure out what was going on. We were climbing real slow, and we were pooping along uphill. I suppose we were maintaining about 180 miles per hour, a bit less than we like to do when heavily loaded and working our way up the hill.

"This guy Powell for some reason just refused to get in where he belonged and I kept rocking my wings back and forth and he kept staying back there. Well, I didn't want him staying all the way back. I wanted that formation neat and tight the way it's supposed to be, both for the bombing run and also for mutual protection from the cross fire of all our guns. Then there wasn't any need to be concerned about radio silence because up ahead of me now I could see the B-25s that sure had failed in their decoy job. Here came those B-25s and right with them there were the Zeros. It was a flying circus and there must have been twenty or twenty-five of them—the most enemy planes I had ever seen all at once up to that time. They were like a swarm of mosquitoes.

"Before I could do anything—slow down for this guy Powell or watch out for him or try to protect him—those Zeros hit us. They came in against us like a whirlwind, and there wasn't a doubt in the world that they would take advantage of Powell being far back. He just didn't seem to realize what was going on. He was 'way back, just ambling along and not taking life too seriously, and they hit him like a ton of bricks. Divine told me after the mission that the world seemed to explode in their faces with cannon shells thumping into the plane and tracers all over the place. And did that Powell ever get back into formation *fast!* He really hugged us from then on, for everything he was worth.

"We went over Lae, pouring the coal to the airplanes, our noses down and grabbing for all the speed there was to squeeze out of the engines. We went across the target at about six or seven thousand feet and dropped our eggs, and the tailgunner—John Engleman—said we were getting some pretty good strikes on the runway. A few bombs had geysered in the water, but most of them were right where they were intended.

"We were going downhill now for everything we were worth, really unwinding, going for that speed that was now so precious. There was one particular point when you made your run against Lae that let you know it was time to head for the deck. First you had to pass 'Rapid Roberts'; you had to get past him. He was a Japanese antiaircraft gunner at the end of the Lae airdrome. He was *good;* he could play an unbelievable tune of fast and accurate shooting with his flak guns, and it was always a matter of holding your breath a bit until you got past him. The Zeros would swing off for those seconds that you had to run the flak gauntlet, and the moment you did, then everything got even wilder.

"We hit out for the water just as fast as we could get those planes to move, and thank God they were the fastest kind of airplanes of their class on wings anywhere in the world—or there would have been a great many people who would never have gotten home. We were going downhill with everything we had and—well, I know it violated all the structural limitations and everything else on the airplane that was forbidden, but we were indicating over four hundred miles per hour, the nose of the airplane 'way down and the Marauder pounding along like there wasn't any tomorrow.

"We couldn't outdive the Zeros, but we were now going so fast that in order to stay with us they couldn't go into their long, wide pursuit curves to set up the best gunnery angles. This threw off their aim and gave us the opportunity to throw some good lead in their direction.

"All the other B-26s had only those little .30-caliber popguns in the waist positions, but ours was a bit mongrelized in the rear. Pat Norton, our radio operator, had thrown away those little .30s and he'd cut a large hatch in the bottom of the side fuselage so that he could have a good field of fire, and he was really cutting into those Zeros with that big gun of his.

"It's too bad we had to turn our planes after making the bomb run, because if we could have kept on going, with everything wide open, no bombs, much of our fuel gone, the Zeros would have been really hard-pressed to keep up with us. But we had to get home, and any time we turned, those Zeros would cut in after the advantage with those 'square turns' of theirs.

"They came after us after we got down to the deck . . . ran with and after us like a pack of howling wolves, snapping and slashing. . . ."

Leading the second formation, Johnny Ewbank at the controls of "Old Timer" . . .

"Those Zeros coming in is the most vivid thing I've remembered through all these years, and I can see it like it took place only yesterday. I saw the B-25s in formation and I knew that this was all wrong because they should have been far away by then. There were those B-25s going right smack across our flight path, and they were much higher than we were and in a long dive to pick up speed. And then I first saw all those Zeros and I couldn't really believe it for a moment. Because right then and there I knew that all our plans had gone completely sour on us, and that all the work for a coordinated air strike had gone up in smoke.

"I turned to Mason Brown on my right and said to him, 'Those 25s are 'way late. And look at those Zeros! They're coming for us down on the left!'

"You know right away when you're in trouble, and we were

in it up to our necks. Because it was all too clear that those Zeros, flying well above us and chewing up the B-25s, had hardly been flying at all, and I knew they must have full tanks. And that scared me. What made it worse is that I knew I would have to keep going right along the way we were moving, for our bombing run—and that meant we were flying toward their home field, and even to the alternate target at Salamaua.

"They hit Krell's formation like a ton of bricks. They were all over them and coming in from the side and the front and whipping through the formation and then they were coming wide open for us.

"Right there I switched from Lae to Salamaua for our target. Krell's formation just bored right on through the Zeros to the primary. We started going downhill now because we had not only the bombing to worry about but getting out of there as well. My objective was to get the formation down *low*. To hell with the precision-bombing run at ten thousand feet. Up there, we were sitting ducks for the Zeros. I wanted to get our bombs out and get low, real low, right down on the deck, just as soon as possible. Down there, we had real speed with this B-26, and we could close off our blind spot which is our belly, and our turret and tail guns could really work on the Zeros.

"So we pulled out the plug and went downstairs for everything we had. Man, we were picking up airspeed with a tremendous clip, really unwinding the altimeter needles and bringing our airspeed to the *Do Not Exceed* limit—and then going right on past.

"We were coming down very fast and this made it tough on the bombardiers. Ed Hansen, my bombardier, was pretty mad about having all his plans shot out from under him, and he and I were talking back and forth pretty fast. He told me to get the damned airplane leveled out for the bomb run, and he didn't give a hang about the Zeros; he was busy. We called the other people in the formation, and we planned a specific altitude to level out and bomb so that bombardiers could set their sights and equipment.

"I don't know how we did it, because those Zeros were all over the place, but we leveled off and Hansen was real happy with the run and we let everything go right on target. I don't know what we did down there that day, but the crews behind us reported a great explosion. A little while later, when we were out of the bombing run, the bays closed, we were diving with all the speed we could get to keep the Zeros off their curving pursuit runs on us. I could see smoke pouring into the sky. Intelligence reported later that we hit a big storage dump and set off their fuel drums. It didn't break their back at Salamaua or anything like that, but when you tear up someone's fuel stores, you sure do help in slowing them down a little.

"But it was right then and there that I forgot everything except getting our tails back to Moresby in one piece. I knew we were in for it. We started running for home with Zeros tearing us up all they could. . . ."

Off Ewbank's wing, Jerry Crosson in "So Sorry" . . .

"I saw those B-25s and at once, in the same instant that I saw them, I knew something or someone had really fouled up this whole mission on us. Because the B-25s were *between* us and the target instead of far away from the Lae airdrome, and there was a swarm of tiny dots all around the B-25s. And looking at the dots and watching them growing larger and larger—well, it was like a daydream or something coming true that you knew was unpleasant, and you couldn't do a thing about it, because those harmless expanding dots in reality were Zero fighters.

"They were up at eighteen thousand feet, working over the B-25s, and then they came straight for us, coming down to where we were at fourteen thousand feet. We were just starting to pick up some speed, but nothing like those Zeros in their dives. They were accelerating so fast you could see them really getting up steam. We got the yokes forward in the cockpit and we all started going downhill. We were real anxious to let the old '26 really unwind and pick up her head to run.

"About five miles out from Lae they plowed in a wild, loose mass right into and through Krell's flight directly ahead.

"I watched them really start chewing at Krell's formation. In the lead position of my flight, Johnny Ewbank saw all this, of course. Suddenly he ordered a change of course. We veered off to the right, away from the attack, and now I knew we were going to try to hit Salamaua. We actually passed right over Lae and the airfield, but we were going downhill like a bunch of locomotives dropping down a mountainside, and there wasn't a chance of our own flight hitting the primary target. We went all-out for Salamaua and the bombardiers were working frantically to set up for the final run, because with a sky full of two dozen or more Zeros there wouldn't be any second chance for us.

"They were all over us and around us and trying to get under us where we were blind, and we were really whipping up the steam and getting up our speed. They were making passes at us from the sides. Toward the field at Lae, they started coming in with some pretty wild frontal passes, their wings and noses blazing, guns and cannon hammering away at us.

"On our actual bombing run the Zeros broke away suddenly and gave the flak crews a chance to get in a few licks at us. It was like leaping from one bed of hot coals into another, with everyone just itching for their turn to work you over. The moment we came out of the bombing run, the Zeros came slicing back in with those frontal and side passes at us, and all this time we were doing our utmost—with all our bombs gone now—to let the B-26s grab for all possible speed.

"When the guns fired . . . from the cockpit you could hear a steady rumble. The whole plane was shaking from the recoil. The rumble came at you from the nose and then up and behind or directly behind, and they merged in and out, and there was all the noise of the engines and propellers and, of course, the kind of noise you always hear and *never* forget. That was the sound of the 20-mm cannon shells from the Zeros as they exploded against us. They sounded like a shotgun blast going off in a bucket of sand that was being held right next to your head.

"You could *smell* the fight. You could smell the guns when they were firing, the powder, and I tried for years to compare just what it smelled like. But the closest thing to it is that it smells just like a subway station in New York; I swear that's just what it smelled like up there.

"There was one particular Zero that spelled trouble. I had watched him lead the attack into Krell's flight, and he flew— that pilot in that Japanese fighter—like we didn't have a gun that could bother him. We were moving off to the right from the northeast coast of New Guinea when again I saw one particular Zero boring in like there was no tomorrow.*

"He kept coming in from three o'clock [from the right] out of a shallow diving turn. He stayed in this turn, really coming in fast, and suddenly he screamed over us with tremendous speed. I'd guess he was maybe a hundred feet or so right over us, no more than that, but perspectives are rough to judge under these conditions. He was a pro; he wasn't wasting any ammunition in that long curve, and he was just a hairsbreadth away from a skid; not skidding, but squeezing all the performance out of that airplane. A real master; he waited for the right moment. You can spot the master at this sort of thing right away. A lot of the rookies would splash their ammo all over the sky, but the pros who'd been around for a while knew just what they were doing. And then in a blur he was gone.

"My top turret gunner—Johnston—had been tracking this same Zero, and he called on the intercom that the Zero had

* As will be shown, this is the Zero fighter flown by Saburo Sakai. Personal identification of its markings as seen by pilots and the crewmen of different planes, the maneuvers flown, and Sakai's own report leave no question but that he is the Japanese pilot involved in these incidents.

suddenly flashed up and down, and twisting like a dervish so that he couldn't track him with his guns. He said that the Zero had slammed into the tail section of Bench's airplane behind us, that there was an awful lot of smoke and debris, and that both airplanes were falling out of control." [54]

Fred Nichols, at the controls of the "Flying Parson" . . .
"The Zeros really slammed into us. That brought on some fancy eyeball activities. You had to keep one eye locked on the lead plane in your formation at *all* times, no matter what, because you were supposed to be glued to him. It was a real job not looking directly at the Zero fighters when they were coming at you from all over the place, but keeping that formation was vital. But there came a sudden moment when *something*—I don't know what; call it sixth sense if you want to—told me to look to my left. I snapped a glance over that way and there was a Zero barreling in directly at us, wide open, and on a collision course. I hauled the yoke back and we grabbed for sky, and in the next instant that Zero was right under me, just a flash beneath us. The next thing I knew, our tailgunner, Lawson Smith, was on the intercom. He reported that the Zero had barely cleared our plane, but had rammed into another ship, and that the B-26 was going down with flames and smoke pouring from it . . ."

Not one of these eyewitnesses to this particular episode in the swirling air fight had the opportunity to see accurately what really was taking place about them. The great speed of the Zero fighters and the Marauders, the whirling maneuvers of the Zeros, the anxiety to try to scan all parts of the sky at once, the hammering of guns, and the impact of enemy cannon shells . . . all these contributed to the variety in reporting the collision.

Here, for the first time—told by the one man who could set the record straight—is the truth. That man is Saburo Sakai . . .
"The engine screamed as the Zero dropped suddenly beneath the enemy bombers. I picked up speed almost immediately in the dive and almost at once I was ready for my next move. The gunners in the Marauders were almost certain to try and lead my airplane, expecting that I was diving to come back up for an attack from below. The B-26s have no belly guns, and they are vulnerable here. However, they were always alert for an attack in this fashion, and by maneuvering their airplanes and using cross fire wisely, they could make up for much of this disadvantage. And if experience was any answer, they would already be swinging their guns around to bear on me—where they thought I would be climbing from below.

"Instead, as quickly as I had sufficient speed, I pulled back sharply on the stick, maintaining full throttle. The Zero leaped upward suddenly, and in a moment I was climbing vertically past the bomber I had selected for my target. My idea was to continue up and over in a loop, and then break suddenly in an attack the enemy would not expect. If I had made my firing pass on the same horizontal level as the bombers I would have only one chance to fire. A miss meant my flying well beyond the Marauders; I would then have to turn and come back against them in a wide pursuit curve. This involved going away from the Marauders, turning sharply—with a loss of speed—and then going to engine overboost to catch them again. All this was virtually impossible—once the Marauder started into the dive the Americans used for their escape maneuver, and got down near the ocean, they flew almost as fast as we could in the Zeros.

"So I came up sharply in the loop, keeping the stick almost full back. At the top of the loop, flying inverted, I snapped the stick back to its full limit of travel. Instantly the Zero broke from the curving maneuver of the normal loop, and the nose jerked sharply downward. I glanced to one side; good! Two of the rookies who had followed me against the formation were flying my wing and duplicating the maneuver. And there were more behind them; that should occupy the American gunners!

"As the nose fell earthward, I kicked left rudder and brought the stick to the left. The Zero came down in a twisting dive to bring me into perfect firing position from above. Not a gun was tracking me from the Marauders. At about a hundred yards I opened fire with the nose machine guns. I was closing very fast and at fifty yards I flicked the cannon switch on and fired both 20-mm cannon. I was still closing, coming in to pointblank range. The pass could not have been better. I saw a continuing series of flashes as the cannon shells exploded steadily around the cockpit, along the wing between the cockpit and engine, and into the engine itself.

"Brilliant flame erupted suddenly from this area; the bomber seemed to stagger as the explosion tore through the airplane. Pieces flew off wildly and the Marauder plunged from the formation. As I broke away from the attack, pulling up quickly to stay in range of the bombers, I watched the blazing Marauder falling like a stone. It swerved in its fall; there was little time, of course, to watch it carefully, but it seemed to come out of the dive for a moment. But only for that moment; it smashed into the ocean and exploded."

The Marauder that Sakai had just destroyed was the "Wabash Cannonball," piloted by Lieutenant Willis G. Bench.[55] Moments later, as the Japanese ace pulled out of his dive and came up and around in a tight climbing turn, he spotted another target: a Marauder bomber falling back from the formation, starting to trail the others.

"Climbing back toward the enemy formations," said Sakai, "I saw one bomber begin to fall back. It was alone; I didn't know if it had been damaged in the battle. Neither did I care—for the one thing that counted was that this trailing bomber was a sure-fire target. At once I rocked my wings— the signal for any fighters near me to follow. I pushed the throttle forward to maximum power and swung to the attack, starting the brief dive before cutting up and over in the loop. The bomber grew larger and larger as I closed the distance . . ."

This particular Marauder had not been hit by enemy fighters. But it was in serious trouble and could not keep up with the bomber formations. Walt Greer and "Mac" McMullin looked out at the lone Zero rushing toward them, and further back, another seven fighters in a wild bunch pounding right along.

"*Now* we really are in for it!" shouted McMullin,[56] as his hands worked frantically among the engine controls.

The "Heckling Hare" was in the worst possible trouble— both from a sudden loss of power and from its naked position in the sky—as eight Japanese fighters rushed toward it.

Saburo Sakai and the crew of the "Heckling Hare" [57] were about to meet.

CHAPTER FOURTEEN

"I'M ALWAYS SCARED UP HERE"

The emergency in the cockpit of the "Heckling Hare" came without warning, but in the instant that it happened the pilots knew they were in bad trouble.

The formation was tucked in nice and tight. In lead position, Dewey Flint and Bill Curry held the "Calamity Jane" * steady as a rock as they watched the Zero fighters scrambling into the formations ahead of them. To Flint's left and rear in number-two position were Fred Nichols and Richards in the "Flying Parson." In number-three position, to the right and rear of Flint, was the "Heckling Hare." Behind and slightly to the right of Greer's Marauder, Howard Hayes and Jimmy Reed held the "Shamrock" in number-four position.

* On the right side of the nose, Curry had painted the name "El Valiente."

Greer and McMullin saw the Zeros hit hard. They were close enough to see the battle developing directly before them. They saw the Zeros race in, watched one Japanese fighter tear up and over the second formation in an unbelievably tight loop, and suddenly pour its fire at pointblank range into one Marauder.

They watched the Marauder suddenly show a bright sheet of flame and smoke; as it fell away from the formation the Zero broke away and began climbing sharply in a tight turn. Events took place now in almost a blur. At about the same time, more Zeros piled into the formation. Greer alerted his gunners on the intercom to be ready for the firing runs of the Japanese fighters.

Suddenly the "Heckling Hare" staggered. The reaction of Greer and McMullin was instinctive. Greer's hand shot out and banged against two toggle switches that controlled the propellers of the Marauder: the need was critical to flick the switch settings from *Automatic* to *Manual*. Greer knew that if he did this at once, he could still maintain fair power control over the airplane. But if he delayed, or missed the switches, they were all as good as dead.

The "Heckling Hare" had unexpectedly lost the use of its right generator. In the Marauder, this was a system that demanded complete operation for full performance. The loss of a generator under normal flight was not critical; it called for emergency procedures, but everything remained under control and the pilot could bring in his machine without too much difficulty.†

But Greer and his crew were not even remotely close to a "normal flight" situation. They were loaded to almost their maximum gross weight, with a full crew, guns and ammunition, a heavy fuel load, and a maximum load of bombs— every pound was critical. The airplane was at fourteen thousand feet when the generator went out and caused a sudden loss of power. The early B-26 model that Greer flew was, under these weight conditions, almost at its maximum altitude and needed all the power it could get from its engines to hold its present altitude and speed.

Greer had moved swiftly in the cockpit to flick the toggle switches into the *Manual* position and prevent any further loss of power—but not fast enough. McMullin slammed both throttles forward and increased the propeller pitch of the left engine to its maximum revolutions per minute to help make up for the power loss from the right engine.

† As noted previously, two Marauders after take-off from Townsville encountered generator trouble and were forced to return. Both B-26s landed without difficulty; one was scratched from the mission and the other took off again after emergency repairs were made.

It was not enough. Abruptly the "Heckling Hare" fell back out of the formation, its speed cut drastically. The pilots looked at one another grimly; they both knew that this was the mission from which they might not return. For they were now a sitting duck for the Zeros.

Jerry Crosson ‡ explained the predicament of the "Heckling Hare" and her crew: "When Walt lost his right generator he was in deep trouble right away. The generators on the Marauder are a balanced system. When he lost the one generator, he knew he could operate with the second one, but he was putting a terrific load on it. With our maintenance—wonderful men restricted to patchwork-and-glue because we were so short of parts—the second generator in any system failure was often taxed so severely that it was likely to burn out quickly. If you lost both—that was the end of the ride. You either landed *at once*, or else you got your chutes on fast and got out of that thing.

"Greer had lost the means of controlling the pitch—and of course, his power output—in the right engine. He switched from auto to manual right away—he was real fast in that cockpit—but not quick enough to keep his power. He had prevented an even worse emergency by his speed, his reaction to the problem. If he hadn't, then his prop might have run away—overspeeded—and in no time at all he would have had a nasty fire to cope with.

"When he switched to manual, he locked the propeller into the same position it was in at the exact second that he hit the toggle. This gave him some control; not much, but better than nothing. For the rest of the flight, however, he had to walk a real tight wire. He could flick the toggle switch momentarily, pulling the props out of the manual—the locked—position. This brought the propeller speed down into a usable range, but it's a tough way to fly. And all the time you know you may lose that second generator at any moment, without warning.

"There was another problem. The top turret—the only power turret Greer had on the airplane—ran off the electrical system. With the right generator out, they lost full use of the turret.

"And from what Walt Greer told me later, they needed that turret, and they needed it desperately."

From the cockpit of his Zero, Saburo Sakai watched the Marauder that had now fallen far back from the formation. He eased the stick forward; at exactly the right moment he hauled back on the stick and brought the Zero up and around through the same looping maneuver he had employed to shoot

‡ Crosson discussed at length with Greer exactly what had happened when the right generator went out.

down the first bomber. The Zero cut short its curving motion at the top of the loop and plunged down, twisting in the sudden, sharp dive to bring the cannon to bear against the cockpit and right engine.

Saburo Sakai:

"The enemy pilot was no newcomer; that was obvious at once. As I dove sharply, working the stick and left rudder to concentrate my fire by the cockpit, the Marauder turned suddenly. Even as I rolled into the position to open fire—and squeezed the trigger for both the machine guns and cannon—the bomber made a sharp turn to the left. Its right wing came up at a steep angle, and the Marauder skidded abruptly.

"The American was good! Even as I corrected on the controls I continued firing, squeezing out bursts. But the cannon shells failed to strike any vital parts of the bomber. I watched the bullets and shells hitting the airplane, but my shots were wide and simply put holes in the wings and fuselage. There was no flame and smoke.

"I was working hard now; the Marauder was impossible to keep in my sights. Instead of flying straight ahead in a dive—which I had expected the American to do so as to pick up as much speed as possible—this pilot elected to try and evade my fire.

"The bomber was weaving and skidding desperately; whoever was at the controls of that airplane flew like he was in the cockpit of a fighter. I had shot down many of the enemy Marauders and Mitchells, but never had I seen a B-26 flown like this. The bomber was literally being kicked and pushed wildly through the air. Even as it dove and picked up speed, it kept up its skidding and weaving maneuvers. Never for a second was it still. I snapped out several more bursts. Again I saw my cannon shells and bullets striking the body and wings of the Marauder; and again there seemed to be no effect!

"By now the seven other Zeros had caught up to me, and they came in with a wild rush, the pilots snapping bursts in a steady fashion against the airplane. The Marauder was being crisscrossed from almost every angle with bullets and cannon shells; a lethal patchwork through which it had to fly. But never for a moment did it cease its wild skidding, weaving motions as the Zeros crowded in closer and closer, like wolves eager for the kill. This quarry, however, could fight back, and the bomber's own guns were spitting flame, sending tracers against our fighters.

"I broke away from my attack and soared over and to the right of the fight. There were too many Zeros in front of me at the moment. I was angry with myself for not having been able to finish off the bomber; I had been in a perfect firing position and the enemy pilot had slipped right out from under my cannon. I planned to race ahead, get back into position, and then come in to the closest possible position. I vowed that plane would not get away from me again.

"But I had failed to watch our altitude—and before my eyes the Marauder rushed into the tops of the broken clouds. At once the pursuing Zeros broke off their curving runs and rushed to a clear patch of sky—the bomber would have to come out of the clouds at that point. I moved the throttle forward; I could hit the enemy with full effect the moment he emerged from the mists.

"Suddenly I regained my senses. Eight Zeros rushing after one bomber—while there were still another ten bombers behind us, attacking Lae and perhaps even Salamaua. I turned to look in the direction of Lae, and saw a formation of Marauders in a shallow dive, pushing at full speed toward Salamaua.

"The devil with that single bomber! Let the other Zeros handle him. I pushed the engine into overboost and rushed toward the American planes already preparing for their bomb run against the Salamaua substation. . . ."

Within the "Heckling Hare," "all hell broke loose," related Claude McCredie, who was in the wide Plexiglas nose compartment of the bomber as Sakai ripped the airplane with his guns and cannon. "We salvoed the bombs to get rid of all that weight—Lae was clearly in sight but it was obvious we could never stay in the air at our height and with a full bomb load. Everything happened so fast it was like a blur. We knew immediately, when the generator went out, that we were in trouble. We seemed to slow down almost at once; you could feel the sudden deceleration. And I could see the other planes pulling away from us, of course. I was getting the bombsight all set up for our run over the target when we staggered a bit. Then in the distance I saw this one Jap fighter coming after us with everything he had, wide open. Behind him there was another bunch. One bomber was already going down, and these were the same group that had hit that formation.

"Suddenly we began to jerk around pretty wild in the airplane. Captain Greer shoved over in a dive; our only chance was to get the devil out of there and get into the clouds. All alone in the sky, with so many Zeros around—well, things just didn't look good for us.

"Greer called over the intercom for us to be ready for the attack. I grabbed the machine gun in the nose and tried to track that one Zero I'd seen coming in at us, but he whipped down, below us, and disappeared from sight. Then someone yelled and we were in a sharp turn to the left, and Greer was trying to get all the speed he could.

"I could feel the airplane going through its gyrations. In the cockpit they were really walking the rudder; side to side in big motions, skidding like crazy, so that we would make a poor target. Then someone yelled, 'Here he comes!' The next second—well, that's when all hell busted loose around us.

"Up front I never saw the Zero that creamed us. All of a sudden we were getting hit all over the place. You could feel the bullets banging against and into the airplane. And those cannon shells; there wasn't any mistake about them! Greer never quit walking those rudders and the yoke, though; we were all over the place, jinking and weaving like mad."

All the men in the airplane could feel the cannon shells crashing into the Marauder; angry clots of flame marked the strikes, and metal protested the punishment. Bullets sang throughout the ship. The first Zero had broken off its attack, but the seven pursuing planes swarmed all around the bomber in a roaring melee, and the gunners aboard the "Heckling Hare" were ripping bursts back against them.

"It was a real tough one," Walt Greer said.§ "They hit us even before we got to the target. I thought we were all set; there was Lae in front of us, real clear. McCredie in the nose was all ready for the run. We could see the Zeros breaking away from the B-25s and hitting the first group of planes.

"Then that generator went out, and we had our hands full up there. I didn't catch the prop control as fast as I would have liked, that was for sure. We lost some power right away. With the load we were carrying we didn't stand a chance of keeping up with the rest of the group. At fourteen thousand feet it was just impossible and—well, we just slid back away from the formation and I knew we were about to get some special attention. Mac in the nose dumped the bombs, and I got the yoke forward and we started a diving turn to the left.

"This one Zero came in fast, but for a moment he looked like he was going to go under us and just keep right on going. All of a sudden one of the gunners yells out that he's coming up, and he's above us—and then he was coming down. I didn't know what was going on at the moment; McMullin looked up and back and he could see him, and he called him coming in. The moment that Mully saw his nose and wings start to flash, I started jinking. Hard! We were picking up speed now that we were going downhill, but it wasn't enough. I was weaving and skidding, real sloppy, but anything to keep that guy off our neck. He splashed a lot of stuff all across us, but nothing that hurt. We caught him off guard, I think, with that weaving.

"And then a whole mess of his friends piled onto us. I was trying for the clouds with everything we had . . ."

§ Conversation between Walt Greer and Jerry Crosson; see note 56.

The Marauder broke into the clouds. For several moments the mists enveloped the airplane. The men sighed with relief; but they knew their respite was only temporary. Greer could not keep diving blindly or he might take the bomber straight into a mountain. And because he could not drop as low as he would have liked to do, it meant that he would be breaking in and out of the cloud cover.

"We got a break when we first dropped into the clouds," recalled Harry Baren. "Back in the tail, looking out, I'd had a nasty scene to watch before the captain ran for the clouds. I didn't know who was hit, but after we turned—we had lost power and were turning—I had a good view of the formations. I saw this one B-26 get clobbered. Man, but he was hit. I didn't know whether or not he had been rammed; I saw one Zero cutting into the formation and then there was an explosion. I could see pieces of airplane, and the B-26 falling, and then I didn't have much time to worry about anything but us because we began to bounce all over the sky, it seemed. Then we were getting hit!

"I never saw that first Zero. There was just this wild evasion we were going through, and I could hear the cannon shells smacking into us; Greer was really kicking the airplane around. In the tail I was going through some wild yawing motions; great big swinging arcs. It was wild.

"And then the others came in and I had my hands full. The seven Zeros were in and out of the clouds with us. They were like a bunch of dogs yapping at our heels. Four on one side and three on the other, and they'd shift, coming over and below us, rushing ahead of us so they could come in from the front, but mainly to get those pursuit curves. That let them have a long firing run; that gave them the greatest period to spray us good. I know I was busy getting that .50 on them.

"I'd cut off the gunsight. Use the tracers; that was the way we'd hose them down. I clobbered a few. Didn't see them go down or anything, and I didn't care. Just as long as I stitched holes in them and they shied off.‖

‖ It has taken more than twenty years to weave together many of the details of this incident, but after bringing together personal reports and data from both the American and Japanese sides, it seems beyond question that Harry G. Baren was the gunner who shot down the Zero flown by Naval Aviation Pilot 2/C Sakio Kikuchi. The Zero, only lightly damaged, was ditched in the sea by its wounded pilot; examination of the body showed wounds from .50-caliber bullets. The turret was virtually out of action and the single .50-caliber gun in the nose had jammed, therefore, Baren's gun was the only .50-caliber weapon firing at this time. Baren never claimed a kill, but all parties involved are convinced that it was he who shot down Kikuchi's Zero.

During take-off, Lyndon Johnson remained seated in the radio compartment. But once they became airborne, he moved around the main part of the airplane where he was able to look out through the small window on the left side of the fuselage. He also stood on a small stool in the center of the fuselage so that he could bring his head up into the clear Plexiglas bubble atop the airplane, from where he could survey the entire scene and watch the other Marauders. On the way to Lae, he was able several times to squeeze his head and shoulders between Greer and McMullin and look forward through the cockpit windshield.

When the Japanese attacked, there was no opportunity to spend time up forward, but by looking through the bubble, Johnson had a spectacular view of the attack. The plane rolled and twisted as Greer dove for the clouds, sawing the rudder back and forth. The airplane was filled with sounds: the thunder of the engine, the shrieking wind, the impact of the Japanese bullets and exploding cannon shells, and the stuttering bark of the machine guns firing in bursts at the Zeros.

Several times during the air fight Johnson worked his way back to the waist guns where Lillis Walker was on his knees, moving back and forth from the left waist gun to the one on the right as the best targets presented themselves.#

The gunners, hammering away at the Zeros, flinching by instinct when cannon shells went off near them, were amazed with the cool reaction of Lyndon Johnson under fire. This was his first exposure to the enemy; it was the kind of situation in which many a man might be expected to yield to great fright, for it is clear that the "Heckling Hare" was virtually being shot to ribbons in the air. The men stated later that they felt their odds of survival were, at the time, "no better than stinking."

The faulty generator did more than cut power to the right engine. Bob Marshall in the top turret had his hands full because of the snarl in the electrical system. With its twin .50-caliber machine guns and excellent field of fire, the turret provided the most important defense of the airplane. Normally, Marshall could swing his guns rapidly from any one point to another to track and to lead an attacking fighter. But when the generator went out, he could move his guns easily up and down, but he had lost all power to swing them in azimuth—around the line of the horizon.

There was an emergency manual system, but it was strictly

Reported Lillis M. Walker about this incident: "He—the Navy officer with us—came back to my position a few times when the going was real rough. He moved through the plane, trying to see everything that was going on."

emergency and not very good at its job. Marshall had to force the gun barrels against a wind of from three hundred to four hundred miles per hour, and this takes brute strength. There was some help through the gear system, but it was not enough. Moving the guns was a tedious and slow task, and the lack of full power for the turret was a calamitous loss in terms of survival.

At the waist guns, Lillis Walker did not even have time to gripe about the hot shell casings that were slamming against his back and neck. As the turret guns fired, the hot casings splashed down against Walker; they had burned him more than once on missions. But on this flight, as Walker recalled, things were so hot he was not that much bothered by a few burns across the back of his neck.

The running fight lasted, according to the best estimates of both the crew in the bomber and the Japanese pilots as reported after their return to Lae, somewhere between ten and thirteen minutes—which is an eternity when a single bomber is being chewed up by a swarm of wild-flying Zeros. And in the nose of the "Heckling Hare," Claude McCredie cursed angrily when the single machine gun at his disposal jammed. He fought to free the .50-caliber gun, but to no avail.

"Greer yelled at me to get out of the nose," said McCredie. "He ordered me to get back in the fuselage right away and to man one of the waist guns with Walker; that way we would have both waist guns going for us.

"The passageway out of the nose is along a real narrow catwalk. You come up from the nose, through the bomb bay, into the radio compartment. The radio and navigator's table are on one side, and there's a little seat on the left. There's just enough room to squeeze by when someone is in that area.

"When Greer yelled for me to get back to the waist gun, McMullin had to push back out of the way to let me out of the nose. I got to the door ledge and came down the two steps into the navigator's compartment. Commander Johnson was there, looking out the window. He could see right out over the wing; there's a pretty good view out there—although at this moment it was the kind of sight that scared you right out of your wits. That's how I felt when I saw a bunch of Zeros pounding in against us.

"When I left the nose, there were a bunch of Zeros, three or four of them, laying out there on the left side. One would fake a pass at us and when we tracked him with the guns, why, the others would come roaring in to rake us good. They would try to drop down and come up real fast to get us in the belly.

"And Johnson was watching this real close. You can't see

too well through that side window if you're sitting down. He was stooped over in a standing position as I came into the radio compartment. He was looking out the window where the Zeros were starting their pass at us.

"He turned to me when I came in the compartment. He lifted his hand and held up three fingers. Then he pointed out the window and smiled. 'There're three out there on the left,' he said.

"I looked out the window, figuring they were still laying off. But they were coming straight at us and firing! And this man was as cool as a cucumber. I took one look at those Zeros . . . the guns and cannon were all firing at us. I just blurted out, 'Excuse me,' and started past him.

"He grinned at me as I went by him as fast as I could, getting back to the waist-gun position."

Harry Baren commented on this: "If we had had another machine gun lying around, this man would have grabbed it and whaled away at the Zeros. It's a helpless feeling just to be in the airplane when the fighters are coming in; you want to do something, to hit back. Ray Flanagan, who used to fly copilot most of the time with us, used to go nuts up in that cockpit. He wanted a gun, or even some rocks to throw at the Zeros—*anything*. He wanted to fight, not just sit there and take it. That's the roughest of all. Johnson had the same feeling all right. He said something to me about wanting to do something, to get a gun in his hands to fire . . ."

McCredie worked his way back to the waist position. Several minutes later, Lillis Walker had to leave the waist gun he was firing to get to the radio compartment. Each time the Marauders flew a mission, they returned with great caution to Moresby; the Japanese had a cute trick of blowing hell out of Seven-Mile Drome even while the Marauders were blasting the Japanese runways. And they had caught some of the American bombers at the worst possible moment. Walker now had to monitor the radio to be sure that Seven-Mile was clear for them to land.

"It sure was rough up there," Lillis Walker said. "We were really getting shot up pretty bad. The Zeros stayed with us, working us over, like they were having a field day with target practice, a long running fight while they kept whacking away at us.

"When I went forward I had to crawl through the bomb bay to get to the radio. And there was this passenger of ours, just as calm as if we were on a sight-seeing tour. I mean that; he was really taking the whole thing as though nothing was wrong. Bullets were singing through the plane all about us and we were being hit by those cannon shells, and he was— well, just calm, and watching everything.

"He was standing on the stool in the compartment; from up there that's a sight to scare the living daylights out of you. A couple of the Zeros were in front of us and coming in, firing everything they had, and you're looking straight into the face of death when *that* happens.

"He had to get off the stool so I could get to the radio. He stepped down and turned to me and said, 'Boy! It's rough up here, isn't it!'

"I just nodded at him.

"Then he asked me, 'You get kind of scared, don't you?'

"Now, that's one question I can answer very easily. I looked him right in the eyes and I said, 'Yeah; I'm *always* scared up here.'

"He burst out laughing at me—I'm sure he felt exactly the way I did, but he just didn't show it. He didn't show it a bit."

The Zeros finally broke off their attack, and a vastly relieved crew let the tension ease from their bodies. Several of the men assembled in the fuselage, and Johnson slipped the chute from his body as the airplane eased toward the ground. Greer was playing the bomber with consummate care, babying the engine, watching the right propeller like a hawk.

Greer brought the "Heckling Hare" in for a beautiful landing, touching down without a jar. The bomber rolled off the far end of the strip and was waved to a parking space. The men climbed down gratefully to stretch.

Lyndon Johnson turned to McCredie. "You know something?" he said. "I am sure glad to be back on this ground."

Then he turned to the crew standing in a group. "I appreciate the flight and being with you," he said. There was a pause. "It's been very interesting," he added. Then he walked away to meet several people rushing up to the airplane.

"We were flabbergasted," Baren said. "He was as cool as ice."

CHAPTER FIFTEEN

RUN FOR HOME

Even as the "Heckling Hare" twisted and rolled wildly in its dive for survival, fighting its long running battle with the Japanese fighters that steadily shot up the airplane, the other battle raged behind them . . .

"After watching Bench's airplane going down trailing flame and smoke," said Fred Nichols ("Flying Parson"), "I can assure you we were more than a little concerned about all those Zeros. They were on our back and beneath us, all over the place, snarling in and around us, and somehow you seemed to forget that you were flying an airplane. We sort of broke slightly from the rest of the formation, but let me tell you we got back in a real hurry. We were falling behind and I poured the coal to the ship to close it up.

"Because if the Zeros caught you when you were behind, they'd cut in against you like maddened hornets. You were wide open and the best possible target to them. So we came back in a real hurry and the next thing I knew I was hugging the belly of another B-26, tucked in real close and tight, and we stayed there until we got down so low that we had to spread out a bit because we were right down on the water, kicking up spray . . ."

Walt Krell, leading the bomber formation in "Kansas Comet" . . .

"They kept hitting us pretty much in the pattern we had come to recognize. These guys would rush up on either side. Or maybe there would be three or four Zeros off on one side and high above us, and then three more Zeros on the other side. The guy at the tail end of all this would have red stripes slanting across his fuselage, and that marked him clearly as the Japanese commander of this particular bunch.

"Now these guys seemed to be dedicated to committing themselves to an attack before getting on home. It looked to us as though the chief of the whole operation was riding herd on them, and heaven help them if they didn't come through us, and one at a time, and no nonsense about really closing in tight to give us a working-over. Anyone who ever said they— the Japanese pilots—were hesitant about coming in through our guns, well, he just never saw *these* Zero pilots. They didn't stop at anything.

"So they came through us, but usually one at a time. We would always take them one at a time, and they never did realize what a break they were giving us. We were able to coordinate our guns and that didn't help the Zero pilot at all to concentrate on *his* attack. If they had ever come through us three or four at a time . . . well, I just don't think we could have hacked the blow. They might have creamed us pretty bad.

"But because they came in so often alone, we concentrated on the attack and we could do something to help ourselves. There were so many times that I can't remember the number . . . but I would sit there in the cockpit, watching a guy commit himself against us. I'd watch him like a hawk, watching him get his guns and cannon started. I'd stare at the leading edge of his wings and suddenly they were blazing with fire and spitting out black smoke and headed right for us— dead-on at us and expanding with frightening speed.

"I'd wait—just grit my teeth and force myself to wait—until the Japanese pilot committed himself definitely. I'd wait until he had so much closing speed on us and was in such a position that he lost all the advantages of his wonderful maneuverability and then, *only* then, I would skid or turn inside his line of flight. And he couldn't do a thing about it.

"The guy would be hauling down, hauling down to get over the top of us, and I'd see our guys working him over, because all the gunners who had him in sight were able to concentrate on him and hose him with tracers while the next guy in a Zero was waiting his turn to come on in against us.

"We'd see the tracers stitching the Zero, but many times they sailed directly over us, and we couldn't really tell what we had done; but we'd see the airplane go skidding over us, and sometimes even when the Japanese pilot was out of gunnery line, his guns would keep on firing into thin air, and a man does that sometimes when he's been hit. It's a reflex. So we don't *know* how many we hurt, or just shot up a bit, or maybe hit so badly they never got home.

"But while all this was going on—pretty much of a madhouse on this mission—there was Sam Anderson to contend with.

"Sam had flown with me before the war, and it was a real pleasure to have him in the ship. He came along with us in the radio operator's seat, down and behind the cockpit. This gave him a chance to look through the navigation bubble atop the fuselage whenever he wanted to. But he fair drove us wild with his enthusiasm about wanting to see everything that was going on.

"Sam kept jumping from the lower position of the radio

compartment; he'd jump up to the cockpit step and then he'd yell, 'Let me look!' or 'Hey! Can I look? Move over!' and he'd try to shove his head and shoulders between us to get as close to the cockpit windshield as he could. He wanted to look out and see as much as possible of the fight.

"He didn't seem to know we were in the middle of a battle, but almost every time he got up there with us and managed to get a really good look outside, we'd be bounced by the Zeros and their guns and cannon would be blazing at us, and Sam would drop right back to the floor. Because it seemed like the Zeros were really coming right at *him* with everything spitting fire. We were all scared—real scared, when you get right down to it. But the instant a Zero flashed by, Sam was there again, yelling to look outside."

"Buckwheat" (red hair and freckles) Westmoreland was turret gunner in "Shamrock," last bomber of the last wave . . .

"We got in a good strike, a row of bombs in a train right across the runway, and then once we got past the flak gun along the shore we went roaring out over the water. Hayes— the pilot—was pulling as much power as we had and we were slanting toward the water in a long, flat dive. The Zeros came slicing in after us and, man, that's when you really appreciate the old 26 and the way she began to cut loose.

"We were really steaming along, and up there in the turret it was a wonderful sight to see how our speed was throwing off the Japanese pilots. They were pushing their Zeros with the throttles firewalled, that was obvious, but by the time they could come down through a pursuit curve to make their firing pass, they would start to fall behind us. So they'd straighten out, and they were pouring smoke from their exhausts trying to catch up and get set again for a firing run. Now that's what pleased us, because every time they'd straighten out in their flight, we could really lead them in the sights and snap out bursts at them. . . ."

The Marauders ran for the ocean waves as fast as the pilots could take them down. Being close to the water was a measure of safety. It closed up the blind spot, kept the Zeros from slashing up from underneath.

"The Zeros would come up in sudden zoom climbs, pouring lead and cannon shells into the belly of a plane; at the top of their climbs the fighter pilots would go through a sharp half-roll onto their backs and then dive away inverted, getting out of range, and recovering. This is what our pilots wanted to prevent, so we went down on the deck and we were pounding along with everything wide open.

"We were so low that the props were sending up two huge whirlpools of spray and water. Each plane looked as if it were being followed by two howling vortexes—which is just what was happening. The lower arcs of the propellers were creating a partial vacuum, and they were sucking up the water and whipping it back. For a while—man! everything sure got wild. The Zeros were all over us. I had my intercom on all the time, I was so nervous. I was talking at a real fast clip but I couldn't hear anybody. You're supposed to flick the intercom on and off, but I was too excited and nervous and scared and I was just cutting away at the Zeros . . ."

What no one knew all this time was that the "Wabash Cannonball" was fighting for its life. The impact of bullets and explosive shells had torn huge pieces of metal from the airplane, set afire the right engine, and blown a chunk off the vertical fin and rudder. The Marauder had plunged from the sky, but it was not yet lost. In the cockpit, Willis Bench and Pilot Officer Passmore were fighting desperately to save their lives. As the bomber fell, they brought the machine out of its careening dive. Then, their speed increasing while they were under partial control, they knew a few moments of hope as they tried to rejoin planes from another formation. But only a few moments, because then . . .

Westmoreland: "I'll never forget that sight—it's still vivid in my mind—of Lieutenant Bench's airplane. He was coming down from altitude with one of the engines really pouring out thick black smoke. And all of a sudden the airplane just plowed—just smashed into the water with tremendous impact. And that was it; it was all over for them . . ."

Also in "Shamrock," riding in the clear, rounded nose, was Tom Cunningham, bombardier and nose gunner . . .

"That's quite a view from the nose when you're right on the deck and pounding along. Tight formation down here is impossible. When you're so low that the props are kicking up water, you've got to watch the water in front of you more than you do anything else, because if you slip just a little bit and the wingtip catches a wave—well, it may hit at the wrong angle and then it's like shoving it into a block of concrete, and the next moment there's a cartwheeling ball of wreckage spewing itself along the water.

"It can scare you to death, but when you're on the nose gun you worry about something else: the Zeros. All I could see of the ocean was a blur; we weren't ten feet off the deck, pounding along, it seemed, like we were about to touch.

"I had just looked off to the right to follow a Zero coming in when I saw another B-26. It was sliding out of the sky, and one engine was pouring out black smoke. It was low; for just a moment I could have sworn it was fighting to stay in level flight, but it wasn't possible to tell all this, of course. Right then and there all my attention went to that Zero which was coming in with everything blazing away.

"And then all of a sudden the shells and tracers were splattering into Bench's airplane, and he was much closer to us than before, and I must have been staring . . . because glass was spraying and I distinctly saw Bench slump forward on the yoke."

Everything was a blur in the next moment. Two things happened almost simultaneously. Cunningham saw the bomber smash with "terrifying force" into the ocean, exploding and disintegrating at the same time. And then, all at once, Cunningham's body jerked spasmodically.

"I thought . . . well, it felt as though someone had shoved a red-hot knife into my back. There wasn't any question about it. I knew I'd been hit, but I didn't know how bad, only that something had cut right into me. . . ."

There were two final acts to be played in the drama of the air battle. The Marauder in the number-four position of the lead formation had been badly mauled by several Zeros. Pierre Powell had paid the price for not staying tight in formation; the Zeros marked the airplane off for special attention in their first passes.

The Marauder was a flying wreck, its wings and body chewed up and looking like a sieve. Powell dove desperately for the safety of the clouds and was free of the Zeros for a moment. Then a single Zero broke out of the pack and raced after him on an interception course.

In that Zero was Saburo Sakai.* He closed in with full speed against the Marauder . . .

"I managed to close the distance rapidly to the trailing bomber in the first group of Marauders. From about one hundred yards' range, I pumped all the 20-mm cannon shells still remaining in the Zero at the bomber. My aim was perfect; I watched the shells striking home and exploding all across the plane. But the bomber continued right on flying! I was amazed; I had hit that airplane with enough cannon shells to have shot down several enemy bombers. But still it flew on. Angrily, I pushed the engine to overboost and closed in rapidly. I climbed and then half-rolled to come down in perfect firing position. The cannon were now empty, but I squeezed out a long burst from the nose guns. This time I poured my fire into the cockpit area. Once again I saw strikes directly where I had aimed.

"I pulled up and—instinctively—scanned the sky all about

* Intensive screening of all combat activities during the air battle, and the confirmation by Sakai that this was the "last plane in the first group of Marauders," plus reports of the B-26 pilots, make it clear that Saburo Sakai was the Zero pilot in this action.

me. Near the coast of Salamaua, I saw a Zero sliding into the water. It seemed to be ditching under control rather than crashing; I hoped the pilot would get out.

"When I turned back again my target was no longer in sight. Instead, I saw only three other bombers racing low over the water, more than a mile from me. There seemed to be no question but the last Marauder had finally gone down beneath that last, long burst into the cockpit . . ." †

But Sakai and his commanding officer were wrong. Although badly ripped and torn, the Marauder was far from being lost. The crew fought their way home, alone in the sky but still flying.

The final act of combat was played out in a drama between two men of steel will: Walter Krell, leading the mission that day, and a man he could not then know and would be able to identify only twenty-two years later. That man was Hiroyoshi Nishizawa.

The Japanese ace was enraged at his failure to score any kills against the Marauders. The Americans had considered themselves safe from further attack when Nishizawa made his final bid for a kill.

Krell and Anderson have both related that they were fifty miles out from their bomb run when suddenly they saw a single Zero diving toward the sea well ahead of them.‡ Close to the water, the Japanese fighter suddenly clawed around in a tight turn, reversed its heading, and then screamed against the Marauder in a head-on attack. The men stared death in the face as Nishizawa in his wild anger kept down his trigger: the nose and wings of the fighter flashed brilliantly as the guns and cannon poured lead and explosives at the bomber.

Krell waited for the Zero to break away, either by slipping close beneath them or by pulling up; he did not expect the latter, since this would have exposed the Zero's belly to the racking fire of the top turret.

But the Zero did not bend from its flight, but roared straight toward the American plane on a collision course.

"I always forced the Zero pilots to break away in any head-on run like this one," said Krell. "And they always did. Every time, even if it meant a last-second drop away from us. But something, I don't know what, set an alarm bell clanging in my head. I don't know why; I just knew that this was one

† Captain Masahisa Saito gave Saburo Sakai credit for a confirmed kill in this action, making it two Marauders for the day.

‡ This fifty-miles-out position was confirmed in the separate reports of both Krell and Nishizawa. Captain Masahisa Saito made available the report of Nishizawa on his return to Lae; it checked exactly in every detail with Krell's mission debriefing report.

Japanese pilot who would play this thing out to a head-on collision." §

Krell slammed forward on the control yoke. Despite their being close to the water, he had no choice but to whip the Marauder into a violent dive. Almost as quickly—as the Zero screamed by only feet (or inches) directly above them—he horsed back on the yoke to keep from plowing into the ocean.

Sam Anderson took a beating during the violent maneuvers. The centrifugal force hurled him upward through the air into the navigator's bubble. The blow was so severe that he thought he had broken his neck. In the next moment, as Krell hauled the bomber upward, the force was reversed and Anderson was slammed in a wild tumble to the floor of the bomber.

But that was the last of it. The fight was over . . .

At Seven-Mile, General Scanlon had watched the "Heckling Hare" sliding down for a landing. The crash trucks and "meat wagons" were at the ready. Scanlon studied the slashed and torn skin of the airplane, mute testimony to the battering the craft had taken. The rough sound of one engine told him immediately that the landing could end in trouble. He was delighted to see Greer bring the Marauder smoothly to earth, and even more delighted to learn that, despite the extensive damage to the airplane, none of the occupants had been injured—much to everyone's astonishment. Sometimes, Scanlon noted, luck works with instead of against a crew.

Mike Scanlon, Lyndon Johnson, Ralph Royce, and several other officers remained in a group alongside the runway as the other bombers began to return to Seven-Mile. An ambulance was alerted to meet the "Shamrock" in order to pick up Cunningham and rush him to the emergency hospital near the field.

They counted nine more bombers, and learned from the other pilots that the "Wabash Cannonball" had gone into the water with terrific impact.

Lyndon Johnson was stunned.

Was there any hope—*any* hope at all—that there might be survivors? Could some of the men aboard the Marauder have escaped? ‖ The men who had seen the crash stated flatly that there was not even a ghost of a chance.

§ This conviction on the part of Krell is the only reason that he, and everyone else in the plane, survived. Nishizawa had sworn an oath to himself not to swerve, even if it meant crashing head-on into the enemy bomber. And he kept his oath; he did *not* veer an inch.

‖ The grasping at straws was not unfamiliar, since "miraculous" escapes had taken place before. General Scanlon's diary for this

And where was that last bomber—with Dwight Divine? All the other planes, save the "Wabash Cannonball," had returned except Divine's Marauder.

The men on the ground studied the sky anxiously. Minutes later came a shattered wreck, limping its way toward the airdrome. The ship was riddled from nose to tail, and the whole belly was torn into wreckage. Walt Krell ran to a Marauder and flicked the batteries on; within a few seconds he was in touch with Divine in the crippled airplane and helping to "talk him down."

Divine was at the controls. "When it became obvious that we couldn't get the gear down on the airplane because of all the damage," he explained, "I took over the left seat. Powell climbed out and gave me the controls, which took a lot of good sense on his part. He'd never bellied in a '26 and I'd done it before and knew what to expect. So we came in gear up. I aimed it away from the steel planking, because if you get caught up in that stuff, you can get mixed up in a big ball of wreckage. I brought it in on the grass-and-dirt area. A highly spectacular feat—but in this airplane about as dangerous a thing to do as biting off a hangnail on your index finger. We didn't even get shaken up."

Along with the others, Scanlon and Johnson rushed to where the Marauder had slid to a halt, dust still streaming down over it. The crew climbed out, grinning.

Scanlon and Johnson talked with Divine about the belly landing, and Johnson remarked, "That's one of the best landings I've ever seen."

Sergeant Claude McCredie was standing in the group that had gathered around the crippled bomber. "Johnson was standing near General Scanlon. A group of the officers were discussing the landing and the mission itself. Johnson turned to someone—I don't remember who it was, the whole group was together—but Johnson said to them, 'You can have this place over here. You people really need some stuff to fight with.' If he was asking about what we needed, I sure know what the answer was—*fighters*. We sure did need them . . ."

Another group of people were rushing down to the runway to the crippled Marauder lying on its belly. If Johnson and Anderson ever required dramatic proof of the desperate need for parts and supplies, what took place next convinced them once and for all.

"Within a few hours after Divine bellied in," related Al Stanwood (pilot of "Pistol Packin' Momma"), "that B-26 looked as if it had slid down a mountainside. Dwight brought the machine in as smooth as silk, and stopped just beautifully.

date, in fact, noted of Stevens: "It is possible but quite improbable that he may not be killed but taken prisoner." But no pilot for a moment believed there were any survivors.

But the word was all over the place that a B-26 had creamed its way in, and all the mechanics and crew chiefs at Seven-Mile came loping onto the scene like a pack of wolves sniffing blood. They were so desperate for spare parts and supplies that even before the dust had settled they were scavenging for parts. They did more damage in a few minutes, tearing off pieces and sections, than had occurred in the emergency landing."

Lyndon Johnson's actions after he left the runway were noted carefully by the crews. Instead of leaving Seven-Mile to rest, after his narrow escape from death, he asked to be taken to the hospital to see the wounded.

"The doctors had dug a tracer bullet out of my back," said Cunningham. "It turned out—happily—that I was hurt a lot less than I'd thought. But I was stunned, still a bit in shock, from the impact of the bullet. I was lying on the hospital bed when I saw a tall Navy officer wearing suntans come in. He walked over to me to talk with me for a while. He was a lieutenant commander; he introduced himself as Commander Johnson, and asked me how I was doing. He was real pleasant and stayed with me about fifteen or twenty minutes.

"I didn't know anything about him except that there were a couple of VIPs along on the mission that day. The pilots told us that they would be in different planes, and to 'show them what we're made of.' We didn't need to do that; the Japanese supplied all the action anyone could ever have wanted."

On the night of June 9 the men assembled in General Scanlon's home, on a hill overlooking Port Moresby's harbor and Seven-Mile Drome, behaved in a subdued fashion. During the evening, as high-ranking officers convened with Generals Royce and Scanlon, and to meet the Congressman from Washington, two men sat off in a corner by themselves. They spoke in low tones, discussing their friend who had died that day. Sam Anderson and Lyndon Johnson for a while remained apart from the large group; finally, Johnson asked that he be left to himself a little longer. Anderson returned to the group.

After dinner the men retired for the night. At Moresby, that meant sleeping along a row of hospital beds placed on the porch of Scanlon's home, each bed surrounded by mosquito netting. The sound of voices fell away quickly. It had been a day long to remember. And take-off for the next morning was scheduled for 7:00 A.M. sharp.

There is a page of history to be rewritten about the mission of June 9. Whatever official records still exist—and these are not in the archives of the United States government—indicate that the Marauders on this mission were credited with the confirmed destruction of thirteen Japanese fighter planes. That record is wrong.

On June 9, 1942, the Japanese fighter wing at Lae airdrome lost two Zero fighter airplanes and their pilots to the enemy. One of these men—Naval Aviation Pilot 1st Class Sakio Kikuchi—was in the Zero that Sakai saw ditching in the sea.

There was another battle in the skies over New Guinea. As the last of the Marauders fled before the attacking Zeros, a group of eleven Bell P-39 Airacobra fighters suddenly appeared near Lae. These fighters were scheduled to provide withdrawal cover for the Marauders, but they failed to arrive in the proper area and they showed up much too late to fulfill their mission.

They did, however, encounter between three and six Zeros over Cape Ward Hunt. Nishizawa had just returned from his abortive attempt to shoot down the Marauder flown by Walt Krell, and arrived at the scene—without ammunition—in time to see the Airacobras plummeting in steep dives against the Zeros. The American fighters made one diving pass apiece and were gone.

Behind them a Zero flown by Naval Aviation Pilot 1st Class Satoshi Yoshino, assigned to the Yamashita Company, fluttered down from the sky in flames. The Airacobra pilots were unaware, of course, that the pilot's name was Yoshino—or that they had shot down a Japanese pilot with fifteen confirmed kills, an ace three times over. None of the American fighters was lost.

It is interesting to note that the Marauders were officially credited with thirteen kills when, in truth, only one Japanese fighter was shot down, by Harry G. Baren, tailgunner of the "Heckling Hare."

The Japanese Zero pilots were officially credited with four Marauders shot down—two to Saburo Sakai and one each to two other pilots (Sakai claimed one Marauder definitely shot down and one confirmed; the other two claimed definite kills). In actual fact, as we know, one Marauder was lost, shot down by Sakai.

The Airacobra fighter pilots claimed two Zeros shot down and "several damaged." Only one was shot down. (The Japanese did not claim any kills of the Airacobras.)

As the men on the porch of General Scanlon's quarters drifted off to sleep, another group of men one hundred and eighty miles away were expressing their emotions at the loss of their men.

As darkness fell over the small military air base of Lae, the pilots and officers of the command post assembled to hold funeral services for the two men lost that day in battle. The fighter pilots of Lae donned their white dress uniforms. Scarlet tropical flowers were brought to the scene in the only containers available at the remote New Guinea outpost: empty beer bottles; incongruous in nature, they were spiritual in purpose. Sticks of incense, considered indispensable for Buddhist funeral rites, simply were unobtainable; the Japanese commander substituted pyrethrum coils (normally burned to repel mosquitoes by producing a thick smoke).

The mourning lasted "until late into the night. Everyone was depressed. The loss of the two men was a severe blow for our small Wing at Lae." [58]

The mission of the ninth of June, 1942, was over.

CHAPTER SIXTEEN

AFTERMATH

During the afternoon of June 9, Frank Kurtz flew the long-delayed "Swoose" into Seven-Mile Drome at Port Moresby,[59] ready to carry the "party of VIPs" back to Australia to continue the tour of military installations. There was one addition to the group when General Royce authorized Barnett of Paramount News to join them.[60]

"The Swoose" took off at 7:15 on the morning of the tenth for the long flight to Batchelor Field, near Darwin. During the five hours and forty-five minutes' flying time[61] to reach Batchelor—home base of the 7th Fighter Squadron—General Royce had the opportunity to continue his long discussions with Lyndon Johnson regarding the combat situation and associated factors within the Southwest Pacific Area.[62]

At Batchelor Field, Anderson and Johnson were provided the means of studying several aspects of the war hitherto unavailable to them, including the defense of Australia itself against powerful Japanese air attacks. They were conducted on a tour of smashed and burned installations by Lieutenant Colonel P. B. Wurtsmith—the same "Squeeze" Wurtsmith who had endeared himself to the Australians by the courageous defense of the continent with a handful of outmoded fighter planes against enemy odds as great as 10 to 1. There was one field in use—an auxiliary fighter base—other than that of Batchelor.

But nothing drove home so starkly the strange and inexplicable behavior of the stevedores in Melbourne and other

Australian cities than the sight that greeted the two Washington observers.

"We visited what was left of the Royal Australian Air Force and the bomber force of the British which had been at Darwin," Anderson said. "There wasn't that much to see. The air forces—the planes and their ground installations—had been pretty well destroyed. The airfield in Darwin itself was a terrible shambles; the Japanese had literally torn the place completely apart. There was every indication of heavy and very accurate bombing.

"Darwin itself had been under attack for a long time. Few people realize just how strong were those Japanese raids. And with the threat of invasion piled atop the devastating raids, the people of Darwin had actually fled the city, moving much further inland. Invasion was something very real to them; we hadn't stopped the Japanese yet in this area.

"The only people to be found in Darwin and the surrounding area were a handful of some of our Air Force personnel and the aborigines, who didn't seem about to move, Japanese or no. We met with the local military people, and I took special note of the fact that they had stressed the total evacuation of every Australian citizen from the area. We were told that there wasn't a single white woman within five hundred miles of there. They had really moved everyone out.

"After lunch we walked outside and we ran right into two complete strangers. Coming toward us was a white man and a white woman; she was dressed in shorts and a man's shirt. They had just arrived in the harbor aboard a small boat. They must have had a terrible time—for they had sailed that little boat by themselves through waters infested by the Japanese, all the way from the Philippines.

"So the official report we were given was just slightly wrong. As of that moment there was a white woman within five hundred miles of us. Just one woman . . ."

On the morning of June 11 "The Swoose," with an additional passenger—Air Commodore F. M. Bladin[63]—took off from Darwin, bound for Cloncurry. It was a long and boring flight across the part of Australia that is open desert, with much the same appearance from the air as the desert areas of Arizona or New Mexico.

The scheduled time of arrival at Cloncurry came—and went. The minutes ticked by, one after the other, and it did not take long for Sam Anderson to realize that something was wrong.

"I had been playing cribbage with a young reporter," Anderson said. "The flight was just long and boring, with nothing to see except desert. Suddenly I realized we were flying squares—the box-search pattern where you're lost and you keep increasing the pattern of the squares you fly in the hope of trying to find out where the devil you are.

"I went forward and asked Frank Kurtz what was going on. There was one radar a long ways off, and a radio station—they were trying to reach anybody who might help to give them a bearing. Kurtz explained that they were lost and they had reached the radar, but the ground station was too far off. They couldn't pinpoint us. There wasn't any triangulation anyway. We were just plain lost."

Sam Anderson was more than a little annoyed at the crew. "Before we took off," he explained, "I looked at the course that they were going to fly. There was a railroad that runs inland from the east coast and I asked the navigator—Schreiber—why we didn't deviate far enough to the east so that we would hit that railroad and have at least one checkpoint for a ground reference. He told me that they wouldn't need that. He was awfully confident. He said, 'When we take off from Melbourne for one of the islands, we don't aim for the island —we aim for the end of the runway.' "

The navigator explained to Kurtz that his octant, used for navigation without ground reference, had gone out on him. Without this instrument (or the railroad checkpoint, Anderson noted wryly) "The Swoose" was completely lost.*

The bomber was rapidly depleting its fuel. Kurtz was more than a little worried about the situation, and he decided to get out of any trouble while he still had full control of the airplane. While it was still daylight (the sun was already near the horizon), Kurtz dropped down to low altitude and dragged several flat areas that looked good for landing. But the ground can be completely different from the way it appears from the air; Kurtz did not want to come barging in and slam the airplane into a gully or a ravine that would smash it up, with the result that his passengers would be "spilled . . . all over Central Australia."

"The Swoose" slipped down from five hundred feet toward a flat expanse near a ranchhouse. "We came in over the trees," said Anderson, "and I could see kangaroos scattering through the trees as we came over and the noise of our engines frightened the animals. We landed with quite a bit of fuel still in the tanks, but that was the only sensible thing to do, of

* General Royce has provided an interesting sidelight to this episode, which, until this book was written, was never made public. He explained that "The Swoose" "had been sent back to Honolulu on a special mission, and it had had all the steel plates in back of the pilots' seats removed. They were later put back in place, but no one remembered to compensate the compasses— the net result of this came to (1) compasses that were badly off, (2) no checkpoints, and (3) we got lost!"

course. It was already five o'clock—we had been flying for eight hours and twenty minutes since take off." [64]

Nearby was the Carris Brook Farm; the owner, Mr. S. H. Taylor, came out to meet them.[65] He sent one of his helpers back to the ranch to bring out hot coffee and milk for the crew and passengers of "The Swoose." Several minutes later, he placed a call to the nearest town—they were forty miles southeast of Winton—and asked for some assistance for the passengers.

It was midnight when the sheriff arrived with several cars behind his own. The passengers left the crew with "The Swoose" and took off on a wild cross-country drive. There was no road to be seen for several hours until, at about three in the morning, they finally bounced their way onto a cross-roads. A tavern was dark and locked tight, but the sheriff aroused the tavernkeeper who, as might be expected, was somewhat startled to see the crowd standing outside his door. However, he readily opened the place and set drinks up for the entire group.[66]

By seven o'clock in the morning they arrived at Winton. The keeper of the North Gregory Hotel set up breakfast for the party, after which they gratefully went to rooms to get some long-delayed sleep. General Royce, before retiring, contacted a supply depot at the town of Long Reach, further to the southeast, and ordered several truckloads of fuel driven to the ranch where "The Swoose" and her crew waited.

Later that day, they drove to a small airstrip near Winton. Kurtz took "The Swoose" off the ranch grounds in expert fashion and slid neatly into the strip at Winton to pick up his passengers. He made a short hop to Long Reach, filled the tanks, and took off again almost at once for Melbourne, arriving there late on June 12.[67]

During the trip with its frequent and lengthy delays, General Royce continued at various times to discuss at length the subject of the war against the Japanese, relationships with the Australians, troubles with communications (which had been demonstrated so dramatically, and repeatedly), and other problems with Lyndon Johnson.

Undoubtedly the tiring effect of the trip, the death of Stevens, and the disrupted sleeping schedule affected Johnson. On this point Ralph Royce sheds some light.

"I did not find Commander Johnson to be particularly affable at this time," Royce explained. "Not as far as I was concerned, anyway. He wanted information, he was driving hard after it, and I could appreciate his viewpoint. That's all there was to it. I answered his questions as best I could, and saw to it that he was made comfortable. The rest of it was entirely up to him. He had a job; he was doing it. I can always appreciate that in any man."

On their return to Melbourne, Lyndon Johnson and Sam Anderson were caught up in several days of briefings and conferences with the staffs of Generals MacArthur and Brett. Johnson and Anderson made reports to the various staff sections of MacArthur's headquarters, and Anderson then went on to Brett's offices, to concentrate on the Air Force side of the war in the second round of meetings.

Anderson made the attempt to see General MacArthur as soon as he arrived in Melbourne, "but I wasn't able to see the general that evening," he said. "After several days we completed our meetings. I still hadn't seen MacArthur.

"I had planned to start my return to the United States on the afternoon of June 18. Early that morning, however—about seven A.M.—General Brett called me directly. He had been thinking, he said, about his communications problems, his organizational setup, requirements to fill out his staff—problems he considered most pressing—and wanted to see me immediately.

"This was all a surprise, since on the afternoon of the seventeenth I considered everything all wrapped up. In fact, Johnson and I were planning to leave on the afternoon of the eighteenth. I'd packed all my clothes, reserved seats for us on a commercial airliner to Sydney, and we were all set to get on that flying boat on which we'd flown down, and start home."

Johnson was still asleep—Anderson saw no need to awaken him—when he left the hotel and hurried to Brett's office. Two hours later—at ten o'clock—Brett's telephone rang. General MacArthur wanted to see Johnson and Anderson at ten-thirty sharp at his office.

Anderson called Johnson and passed on the request; they agreed to meet outside MacArthur's office. When Anderson arrived, Johnson—in full uniform—was waiting for him. They entered MacArthur's office together and were waved to seats.

General MacArthur was disturbed about the mission flown against Lae. He was explicit on the matter. He said he could understand why Colonel Anderson made the flight: since he was an Air Force officer, this type of action was his primary interest. MacArthur made it clear that he knew that Anderson had even flown with the 22d Bomb Group in the United States before the war.

But he also made it clear that he could not fathom the reasons behind Johnson's and Stevens' flying the same mission. General MacArthur then made a particular point of the fact that Johnson—a personal emissary of the President and a Congressman as well—had risked his life on such a dangerous mission. The risks had not been unknown; Johnson had been well aware of them, and the general was at a loss to understand the compulsion behind Johnson's obvious risk of his life on a mission on which he had absolutely no need to fly.

Johnson explained to MacArthur that these men were aware that he was a Congressman from Texas† and that this accentuated his need to (1) see exactly what they had to face and (2) to let them know that their own Congressman was willing to share with them the dangers of their responsibilities.

Nothing more was said. General MacArthur accepted the explanation by Johnson and dropped the subject completely.

Their meeting went on for another hour. MacArthur listened closely to their observations about the survey trip, breaking in only to ask questions about specific points.

They were about to leave when MacArthur announced abruptly that he had awarded the Distinguished Service Cross to Colonel Stevens. Then he rose to his feet.

"I am awarding each of you the Silver Star," he said. He was silent for several moments. Then he added, "I have no medals to pin on you. The citations are not yet completed. But you can pick up some ribbons on your way out, through my outer office, and put those on." [68]

The two officers saluted and took their leave.‡

Lyndon Johnson's flights in military aircraft had been flown somewhat less than as planned or scheduled, and his return to the United States was no exception. Johnson and Anderson departed Melbourne on June 18 and remained in Sydney overnight, planning to take off on the morning of the nineteenth in Admiral Ghormley's PB2Y-2 Coronado flying boat, which was waiting for them in the harbor.

But for the next two days the weather was so foul, with high winds and rough seas, that the pilot of the Coronado dared not risk a take-off. This gave both men the opportunity to rest and to catch up on their notes for their respective reports to be given upon their return in Washington, D.C.

On the morning of the twenty-first, the Coronado lurched through choppy waters to a rough take-off, beginning the flight of eight hours and forty-five minutes nonstop to Nouméa, New Caledonia.[69]

The preceding weeks suddenly took their toll of Lyndon

† None of the members of the 22d Bomb Group, including its commanding officer, Dwight Divine II, with whom the authors have conferred, were aware that the naval commander was also a Congressman. They recall that Johnson made every effort not to ask for special favors, but "went along just like anyone else."

‡ Contemporary reports of this incident have expanded the scene somewhat so as to create the impression—a mistaken one—that a more official and elaborate ceremony took place. No such ceremony was held in MacArthur's office with Johnson and Anderson.

Johnson. By the time the flying boat landed in Nouméa, Johnson was running a fever and was down with what he insisted was only a cold. But the Navy doctors at Nouméa, alarmed with his condition, ordered him brought aboard a submarine tender in the harbor. He spent the night in the tender's sick bay.

The next morning—June 22—Anderson prepared to continue the long trip home. Still ailing, Johnson insisted that he was going with him. The doctors argued with him and warned him that he was courting a much more serious illness; Johnson waved aside their objections. He had to return to the United States and report to the President, he insisted, and he was not about to let any cold stop him. The doctors filled him with medicine in an attempt to reduce his temperature, and against their wishes he was taken to the flying boat.

One hour later there was no question as to the truth of the doctors' warnings. Lyndon Johnson was seriously ill, shaking badly with a chill and a high fever. Anderson and a crewman wrapped him heavily in blankets. The pilot wanted to return to Nouméa, but Johnson insisted—demanded—that they continue on to their destination, which was Suva in the Fiji Islands.

By the time they landed there, Johnson's condition had worsened. Sam Anderson rushed him to a hotel, placed him in bed, and called for a doctor. Several hours later, Johnson was delirious. Alarmed at the condition of his friend, Anderson contacted New Zealand Freedom Hospital. The doctors who examined Johnson declared him so seriously ill as to be almost critical, and brought him as quickly as possible to the hospital.

A few hours later, they managed to bring him out of his delirium. Johnson's persistence in demanding to be permitted to continue the trip back to the States was an attitude the doctors found commendable, but one with which they found it impossible to agree. Commander Johnson, they stated in no uncertain terms, was to remain in the hospital for an undetermined length of time. His condition was grave, and should he even attempt to leave, they would not be responsible for his life.

On June 23, Anderson visited Johnson in his hospital room. He told Johnson that he was continuing on to the States; was there anything he could do for him? There was: Johnson asked Anderson to please call on Admiral Chester Nimitz when he got to Pearl Harbor and inform the admiral of his (Johnson's) whereabouts, and brief him on his condition.

Anderson flew on to the Hawaiian Islands (with one stop at Canton Island), arriving on June 25. He carried out Johnson's request and, early the next morning, continued on his way to the United States.§ It was a rugged trip for Anderson; aboard the famed "China Clipper" flying boat, he had a flight through "wild and rough" weather that lasted sixteen hours and forty-five minutes.

On June 28, Sam Anderson arrived in Washington—the long mission for him was ended.

CHAPTER SEVENTEEN

REPORT

The doctors sent to Suva by order of Admiral Nimitz felt that, after several days of special medical care in the hospital, Lyndon Johnson was well enough to be flown to Pearl Harbor. As soon as he arrived at the huge naval base, he was moved to the hospital at Pearl for further treatment.

The lieutenant commander, resting from his pneumonia attack, was unaware that during his absence, in the spring of 1942, more than twenty-two thousand qualified voters had filed his name as a candidate for re-election in the Tenth District of Texas. With the petitions went this notice:

"It is the overwhelming sentiment of the voters that Lyndon B. Johnson should again be nominated for Congress."

No one even tried to run against him.

On July 16, 1942, Lyndon Johnson removed his uniform and was officially released from active duty with the Navy. President Franklin D. Roosevelt ruled that all Members of Congress serving in the military services were of greater value to their country by carrying out their duties as elected representatives of the people, and ordered these men back to Washington.

Congressman Johnson was twenty-eight pounds lighter on his return to the House than when he had left nearly eight months before. It took a long time for him to overcome the effects of his serious bout with pneumonia.

As soon as it was possible to do so, Johnson reported on the trip personally and in great detail to President Roosevelt. Their first meeting, in late July of 1942, lasted for four hours.

§ Admiral Nimitz, after thanking Anderson for his report, ordered a flying boat with a doctor and medical personnel, plus special foods, rushed at once to Suva for Lyndon Johnson, whose condition was still serious.

Johnson's appraisal—as "the Boss" expected of him—was blunt and straight to the point.

There were other places for his voice—and his knowledge, gained at first hand—to be heard. He took the floor of the House; his voice was heard in the Congress and throughout the United States. He spoke with blunt—often shocking—honesty. He warned that despite all that was being shouted about smashing victories by our forces, it was still possible for the United States to lose the war.

What he had learned from his own personal observations caused him to lash out at the ineffectiveness of certain high-ranking brass.

"We must get rid of the indecisive, stupid, selfish and incompetent among our generals, admirals and others in high military positions," he stated. "We must make it clear that it is no longer a crime to cut red tape.

"We are going to have to give our men leadership and equipment superior to that of any in the world. We are going to have to move quickly to coordinate dive bombers and domestic politics, tanks and military strategy, ships and the will of the people. Management and manpower are going to have to be closely woven into a smoothly functioning machine devoid of departmental squabbles and petty jealousies. . . .

"While we have fighting to do abroad, we have scrapping to do at home. Scrapping of deadwood in thinking, of inefficiency in methods—yes, and of ineffectiveness in men, men who have become entrenched in power, men who love their country and would die for it, but not until their own dangerously outdated notions have caused others to die for it first."

He spoke also of the weapons with which our men were fighting.

"We needn't fool ourselves about the invincibility of our pursuit ships," he stated flatly. He warned that the Japanese Zero fighters were "tough babies to handle." The Japanese had, he said, "a real fighter plane, and we have a long way to go before we can rear back and rest on our laurels. So far as our fliers are concerned, I only want to say this: If we get them the goods, they will deliver. Our men are extremely capable. However, we shouldn't overlook the fact that we are sending a great many pilots up now who are less experienced than the Japanese pilots. . . ."

Although he had flown into combat with the members of the 22d Bomb Group—who raved about the ruggedness and performance of their Marauders—Johnson took special pains to report on the pilots and air crews of the United States Navy:

"We must agree that those Navy pilots can more than hold their own in any fight. However, I do want to say this—that

I'd just as soon try to weather a storm riding on the tail of a box-kite as I would to face the fighting Jap Zero with one of those Navy PBY crates some of those boys are now flying."

The pilots and the gunners, the bombardiers and the radio-men and the navigators of the 22d Bomb Group would all agree:

This Congressman knew whereof he spoke.

NOTES AND SOURCES

1. *Congressional Record* (December 11, 1941), p. 9665.
2. *Ibid.*
3. *Official Biography of Commander Lyndon Baines Johnson, USNR* (United States Navy Office of Information, Biographies Branch) (October 17, 1960).
4. Files and Records, Commander-in-Chief, United States Fleet and Chief of Naval Operations.
5. *Official History: New Zealand in the Second World War 1939-45* (War History Branch, Department of Internal Affairs, Government of New Zealand).
6. *Ibid.*
7. Booth Mooney, *The Lyndon Johnson Story* (Farrar, Straus and Company, New York). Copyright 1956, 1963, 1964 by Booth Mooney. Reprinted with the kind permission of the publisher and the author. Booth Mooney has known President Johnson since 1952, and for six years, during the time the President was a Senator, Mr. Mooney was his executive assistant.
8. *Ibid.*
9. *Official History of the AAF in World War II* (Washington, D.C., 1948), I, 410.
10. *Ibid.*
11. Meetings (tape-recorded and transcribed) with former operations officers and combat personnel of the 22d Bomb Group, AAF, on active duty in Australia and New Guinea, March, 1942 to August, 1944. Many of these officers, during a final meeting with the authors on January 18, 1964, produced personal diaries, general orders, and official operations logs in which their comments had been entered at the time, under the conditions described.
12. *Official History of the AAF in World War II*, Vol. I.
13. *AAF Historical Study No. 9: The AAF in Australia to the Summer of 1942* (United States Air Force Document No. 3-2674-1C, Washington, D.C.; Declassified, 1958).
14. *Ibid.*
15. *Official History of the AAF in World War II*, Vol. I.
16. *AAF Historical Study No. 9.* Also, conversations of Brett with personal friends, as noted at the time in diaries, records, and logs and generously made available to the authors.
17. *Ibid.*
18. *Ibid.*
19. *Ibid.*

20. *Australia in the War of 1939-45* (Australian War Memorial).
21. *Ibid.*
22. Conferences with General Samuel E. Anderson, USAF (Ret.), in Washington, D.C., on December 12, 13, 18, 30, 1963, and January 10, 1964. Extensive reference material, including personal diary and official logs and reports—including General Anderson's flight time-and-missions logs—plus other and extensive reference material, were studied during these conferences. The authors stress that such material was exhaustively cross-checked and compared with similar material from a number of other general officers, and high-ranking officials and personnel. All references throughout the remainder of the book that pertain to General Anderson stem from the above-listed and identified sources and references.
23. *Ibid.*
24. *AAF Historical Study No. 9.*
25. *Ibid.*
26. *Ibid.*
27. *The Lyndon Johnson Story.*
28. *Congressional Record*, April 30, 1941, Appendix, pp. A1992 and A1993.
29. *AAF Historical Study No. 9.*
30. *History of the 67th Fighter Squadron (Single Engine)—Activation to Early 1944.* These records, discovered in late 1956 "in a very worn and badly decomposed condition," had been lost for many years and until now—following their restoration in 1957 by Richard A. Long, Base Historian, 18th Air Base Group—have been unavailable to the general public.
31. Conferences with Major General Ralph Royce, USAF (Ret.).
32. Top Secret Report filed by Captain Carey L. O'Brien, Intelligence Officer, 19th Bomb Group (B-17).
33. *AAF Historical Study No. 9.* Also *Official History of the AAF in World War I*, Vol. I, and other documents.
34. Discussions, tape-recorded, with officers and men of the 2d and 19th squadrons, 22d Bomb Group, in December, 1963, and January, 1964.
35. Letter of January 20, 1944, from Colonel Louis W. "Tad" Ford, USAF, Richards-Gebaur Air Force Base, Missouri.
36. Walter Krell also provided details of Zeamer's sleeping habits under the worst of combat conditions; it is one of the most amazing episodes ever written of a man who went on to win the nation's highest award for valor "above and beyond the call of duty" while piloting a B-17 in "flying wreck" condition over Buka.
37. Notes in flight log/diary of General Samuel E. Anderson, reference to Anderson's conversations with Major General William F. Marquat, June, 1942.
38. Meetings with Saburo Sakai, Tokyo, Japan, 1954, 1955, 1963, and 1964, with Fred Saito. Also *Samurai!* by Saburo Sakai with Martin Caidin and Fred Saito, by permission.
39. Diaries and group records of the 22d Bomb Group.

40. The Japanese side of the war—especially with regard to the missions flown from the field at Lae, New Guinea—are the result of several years of intensive research and study by Martin Caidin and Fred Saito, the latter an ace newsman of Tokyo, Japan. Every surviving fighter pilot of the Southwest Pacific, every surviving officer and commander among the Japanese forces, was interviewed in exhaustive sessions. All surviving records of combat organizations were provided to Martin Caidin and Fred Saito by the Japanese government, including the secret files of combat missions—released for the first time for the purposes of this research. Masatake Okumiya, who fought in more naval air engagements than any other Japanese officer, worked for several years in providing assistance for this material; as did Jiro Horikoshi, the brilliant engineer who designed the Mitsubishi Zero fighter. All combat records, personal diaries, and mission order-of-battle documents were made available as well. This material was exhaustively cross-checked with American files, with pilots and crewmen, and with personal flight logs and diaries. Members of the 22d Bomb Group were asked to make the most intensive study possible of their own records against those of the Japanese. Many of these same pilots, who are involved in the telling of this story in this book, have stated to the authors that the Japanese records, appearing in personal documents obtained for this book, and also in the form of the books *Zero!* and *Samurai!*, are "the most accurate records we have ever seen, anywhere, of this portion of the air war in the southwest Pacific." These statements were made *for the record*.

41. Pat Robinson, *The Fight for New Guinea* (Random House, New York, 1943).

42. *History of the 67th Fighter Squadron.*

43. Official logs and records of 22d Bomb Group for this period supplied by Lieutenant Colonel Dwight Divine, II; John Richardson; John N. Ewbank, Jr.; Gerald J. Crosson; Walter A. Krell; Walter Gaylor; and other surviving members of the Group. Approximately thirty individual collections of records, including official squadron diaries, aircraft logs, personnel reports, damage reports, and extensive other documentation, as well as more than one thousand photographs, provided the background with which to obtain detailed and cross-checked individual reports from participating personnel.

44. Daily report logs of 2d, 19th, 33d squadrons of 22d Bomb Group; Mission Reports and Aircraft Availability and Commission Reports of Operations Officer, Headquarters, 22d Bomb Group.

45. Entry of June 8, 1942, in the personal diary of Major General Ralph Royce: "Went to hotel and had a drink with Marquat, Commander Johnson, Congressman from Austin, Texas, Colonels Anderson and Stevens, also Colonel Connolly . . ."

46. Personal diary of Lieutenant Colonel Dwight Divine II.

47. Interviews with Saburo Sakai, Tokyo, Japan.

48. Personal diary of Major General Ralph Royce. Entry of June

9, 1942, includes: ". . . we took off from Townsville in a B-17E with Lewis piloting because Kurtz hadn't yet brought the Swoose. I had on board the B-17E Courtney, Perrin, Marquat, Stevens, Anderson, Johnson, my aide Kennedy and Col. Divine. It was very crowded and some of them slept on the floor."

49. Personal diary and official reports logs of Brigadier General Martin F. Scanlon, USAF; meetings with General Scanlon, New York, Washington, 1963-64.

50. *Ibid.* Part of the diary entry reads: "Royce and party arrived at about 8:00 A.M. The party consisted of Royce, Marquat of antiaircraft artillery, Colonel Perrin, Colonel Anderson, Colonel Stevens, Commander-Congressman L. B. Johnson, Bill Courtney of *Collier's.* . . ."

51. Conversation in the summer of 1942 between Congressman Lyndon B. Johnson (after his recall from the Navy to the Congress) and the widow of Colonel Stevens, as related to the authors.

52. Letter of April 4, 1962, from Harry G. Baren to The Honorable Lyndon B. Johnson, Vice President. Baren recalls in this letter (which Lyndon Johnson acknowledged) the parachute incident and describes ". . . how small it was on you and how you had to sit hunched all the way. We gave you the business that day, but, you seemed to be relieved when we told you that if we got hit, you wouldn't need a parachute—just a shovel to dig you out. Kidding you this way seemed to help us calm our own fears which were just as great as yours."

53. Secret diary of Naval Aviation Captain Masahisa Saito, commander of the Tainan Wing at Lae, New Guinea, and meetings with both Captain Saito and Commander Tadashi Nakajima. The diary was deciphered and translated for the authors.

54. At least a dozen eyewitnesses of this scene reported that the Zero, flown by Saburo Sakai, had collided with the vertical tail section of the Marauder flown by Lieutenant Willis Bench, and carrying Lieutenant Colonel Francis R. Stevens. All these reports subsequently proved to be incorrect. Lieutenant Gerald J. Crosson later stated: "It wasn't until we landed back at Moresby that I learned that there hadn't been a collision after all. At the mission debriefing we got several eyewitness reports that the Zero had closed to point-blank range, firing with everything he had, and in the explosion that followed, the Japanese fighter broke away clear. A couple of the guys saw Bench's airplane hit the water and explode from the impact— it's like flying into a mountain—but no Japanese airplane went down anywhere near it."

55. Aboard the "Wabash Cannonball" were: Lieutenant Willis G. Bench (pilot), Pilot Officer L. Passmore, R.A.A.F. (copilot), Lieutenant H. P. Beck (navigator), Pfc A. Makuch (bombardier), S/Sgt. Sam Siegel (radioman-gunner), Pfc R. A. Rockefeller (top turret gunner), Pfc G. H. Miles (engineer-tailgunner), and Lieutenant Colonel Francis R. Stevens (observer).

56. The observation and remarks, and the actions, of Walter H.

Greer and Flight Sergeant G. A. McMullin, R.A.A.F., during
this mission were obtained from other members of the 22d
Bomb Group, with whom these two men discussed the events
of the battle. Gerald J. Crosson, a close friend of Walter
Greer, was extremely helpful in this regard, as were members
of the crew of the B-26 Number 01488. Walter H. Greer died
in 1944 at Barksdale Field, Louisiana, in the crash of a B-29
bomber. Flight Sergeant McMullin was lost in action in the
Pacific on June 14, 1944 (confirmation from Headquarters,
R.A.A.F.), and later was listed officially as dead.

57. Aboard the "Heckling Hare" were: Captain Walter H. Greer
(pilot), Flight Sergeant G. A. McMullin, R.A.A.F. (copilot),
Lieutenant Billy B. Boothe (navigator), Sergeant Claude A.
McCredie (bombardier), Corporal Lillis M. Walker (radioman-gunner), Pfc Robert Marshall (top turret gunner), Corporal Harry G. Baren (engineer-tailgunner), and Lieutenant
Commander Lyndon B. Johnson (observer).

58. Diary of a Japanese fighter pilot assigned to Lae, New Guinea.

59. Diary of Brigadier General Martin F. Scanlon, entry of
June 9, 1942.

60. Conference with Major General Ralph Royce; diary reference.

61. Flight log of Sam Anderson.

62. Diary entry, Major General Ralph Royce: "I had many
talks during this trip with Congressman Johnson regarding
the military situation."

63. *Ibid.*

64. Flight log of Sam Anderson.

65. Diary of Major General Ralph Royce.

66. Diaries of Anderson and Royce; also conversations with
Anderson and Royce, Washington, D.C., and Florida.

67. *Ibid.*

68. Conversations with Sam Anderson; reference notes made for
this date by Sam Anderson during return flight from Australia
to the United States.

69. Flight log of Sam Anderson.

INDEX